Teacher's Classroom Guide
To Robert Stanek's Ruin Mist
2nd Edition

REAGENT PRESS
RUIN MIST PUBLICATIONS

Teacher's Classroom Guide
To Robert Stanek's Ruin Mist
Based on the novels written by Robert Stanek

Copyright © 2005 by Robert Stanek
Copyright © 2005 by Reagent Press
Copyright © 2005 by Ruin Mist Publications

All rights reserved, including the right to reproduce this book, or portions thereof, in any form. Printed in the United States of America.

Ruin Mist Publications
Published by Virtual Press, Inc.

Cover design & illustration by Ruin Mist Publications
ISBN 1-57545-038-0

Ruin Mist Publications grants classroom teachers the right to reproduce copies of materials from Ruin Mist in Schools, Review Questions for Discussion, Quizzes and Post-Reading Activities sections of this book for classroom use only. No other part of this publication may be reproduced in whole or in part.

The reproduction of any part for an entire school or school system is strictly prohibited. No part of this publication may be transmitted, stored, or recorded in any form without written permission from the publisher.

Books by Robert Stanek

Ruin Mist Chronicles
Keeper Martin's Tale, Book 1
Elf Queen's Quest, Book 2
Kingdom Alliance, Book 3
Fields of Honor, Book 4
Mark of the Dragon, Book 5

Sovereign Rule

Stormjammers

Young Adult Books by Robert Stanek

Keeper Martin's Tales
The Kingdoms & the Elves of the Reaches
The Kingdoms & the Elves of the Reaches II
The Kingdoms & the Elves of the Reaches III
The Kingdoms & the Elves of the Reaches IV
In the Service of Dragons
In the Service of Dragons II
In the Service of Dragons III
In the Service of Dragons IV

Ruin Mist Tales
The Elf Queen & the King I
The Elf Queen & the King II
The Elf Queen & the King III
The Elf Queen & the King IV

Magic Lands
Journey Beyond the Beyond
Into the Stone Land

Ruin Mist Heroes, Legends & Beyond
Magic Lands & Other Stories

CONTENTS

AN INTERVIEW WITH ROBERT STANEK..10

Meet Robert Stanek... 11

Family and Childhood 12

    How many brothers and sisters do you have?   12

    Did bullies ever pick on you?   12

    Tell me about your Big Brother.   12

    Did you read a lot when you were a child? 13

    Did you want to be a writer back then?   14

    Did you have any pets when you were little?   14

    Tell us about your father and mother.   15

    Did you always do as you were told?   16

    Tell us about your grandparents.   16

    Why did you move to the country? 17

    Tell us about the farmhouse and growing up in the country.   18

    What else do you remember about living there?   18

    What was it like not having your father in your life?   19

School Days.. 20

    Tell me about your first school.   20

    Tell me about your walks to school.   21

    What do you remember about that school? 21

    Tell us about moving and changing schools.   22

    Who was your favorite teacher?   23

    Was there anything you didn't like about school? 25

    Outside of school, what was your childhood like? 26

    Have you ever gone back to the schools you attended?   27

    Did you really get leaches all over you one time? 27

Did you watch a lot of television? 28

Do you miss those times? 28

A car hit you when you were young. What happened? 29

Military Career 30

Why did you join the military? 30

What do you remember about basic training? 32

Was language school hard? 32

Where did you go next? 33

Did you like living in Texas? 34

Tell me about your first assignment. 35

Did training end once you got to your first assignment? 36

Did you travel in Japan? 37

Did you learn Japanese? 37

Did you study martial arts? 38

Where did you go after Japan? 38

Was survival school really scary? 38

Is it true you met your wife while going to flying school? 40

What was Germany like? 40

Tell me more about the food in Europe. 41

Did you travel in Europe? 41

How come you had to go to war? 42

Was it scary? 42

Tell me about Hawaii. 43

What made you want to get a degree, finally? 44

Why did you leave the military? 45

Writing Career 47

When did you first start writing about Ruin Mist? 47

When did you first try to get the Ruin Mist books published? 48

What happened after your first book was published? 49

Tell me about the publication of the first Ruin Mist book. 50

How many Ruin Mist books will there be? 50

What will you do when you publish the last Ruin Mist book? 51

THE RUIN MIST BOOKS 52

An overview 53

    Who are the main characters?   53

    How does the author manage so many characters?   54

    How come the Ruin Mist world has differing histories?   55

    What is the dark place Vilmos visits?   55

    Where do the dragons and titans live?   55

    How come men and elves are enemies in Ruin Mist?   56

    What is the significance of the Ruin Mist book covers?   56

    What is King's Mate?   59

RUIN MIST IN SCHOOLS 61

    Exploring Ruin Mist in the Classroom   61

    Expanding Vocabulary   62

    Learning Creatively   70

    Playing King's Mate in the Classroom   71

    Exploring Common Trades in the Kingdoms   75

REVIEW QUESTIONS FOR DISCUSSIONS 88

Review Questions for Discussion: Chapters 1-2 89

Review Questions for Discussion: Chapters 3-4 91

Review Questions for Discussion: Chapters 5-6 93

Review Questions for Discussion: Chapters 7-8 95

Review Questions for Discussion: Chapters 9-10 97

Review Questions for Discussion: Chapters 11-12 99

Review Questions for Discussion: Chapters 13-14 101

Review Questions for Discussion: Chapters 15-16 103

QUIZZES 104

Quiz!: Chapters 1-2 105

Quiz!: Chapters 3-4 106

Quiz!: Chapters 5-6 107

Quiz!: Chapters 7-8 108

Quiz!: Chapters 9-10 109

Quiz!: Chapters 11-12 110

Quiz!: Chapters 13-14 111

Quiz!: Chapters 15-16 112

POST-READING ACTIVITIES 114

Sorrow & Grief 115

Responsibilities 116

Eavesdropping 117

Friendship & Loyalty 118

Perceptions & Misconceptions 119

Write a Journal! 120

What's the Main Idea? 121

Be the Character! 122

What's in a Personality? 123

An Interview with Robert Stanek

Meet Robert Stanek

Robert Stanek was born in Burlington, Wisconsin. His father was an entrepreneur who immigrated to America from Budapest, Hungary. His mother is the granddaughter of French and Norwegian immigrants. He attended various schools, and joined the United States Air Force at the age of 19. He served in the Persian Gulf War, and earned many medals for his wartime service, including the highest-flying honor, the Air Force Distinguished Flying Cross. After the war, he attended university, earning his bachelor's and master's degrees in only 3 years.

As a boy, he dreamed of being a writer. In elementary school, he was a junior editor for the school newspaper. Although he has written many books for professionals since 1994, his works of fiction have quickly become his most popular books. His first novel was *Keeper Martin's Tale*, which was simultaneously released in adult and children's editions. He describes the book as "a story of mystery, intrigue, magic, and adventure." Many of his other works of fiction are also fantasies, set in incredibly fantastic worlds.

Teacher's Classroom Guide: An Interview with Robert Stanek

Family and Childhood

How many brothers and sisters do you have?

I was the fourth child of five and the only boy. My oldest sister was a teenager when I was born. We lived in a small, green, 2-story house in the city then. I remember she didn't like me going into her room. She could be mean sometimes if she thought I was bothering her.

But she wasn't really mean. I think I just pestered her a lot. When I started kindergarten, she would walk me to school to make sure I was okay. Big sisters are like that. They want their privacy and they don't really mean to hurt your feelings.

Did bullies ever pick on you?

My neighborhood was tough. My mom never wanted us to walk alone. We had a lot of bullies in our neighborhood.

If you weren't a fighter, you'd better be a runner. I was a scrawny kid so I learned how to run fast. The problem is you couldn't always run. I remember my bicycle was stolen one year while I was playing with friends. The bicycle had been a gift from my Big Brother and it meant the world to me.

Tell me about your Big Brother.

My siblings are all girls, so I never had a brother. Big Brothers Big Sisters is a volunteer, youth-services organization. I was something of a whiz kid. I took the standardized tests in the 4th grade. I think that was the first time I'd ever been tested like that and the results that came back astonished everyone. It was a real Malcolm-in-the-Middle moment and you could say the character of Malcolm is a lot like I was at that age. The teachers wanted to advance me to the 6th grade but my mom wouldn't let them. She didn't want anyone to give me special treatment. Looking back, I think that was a good thing.

Anyway, it was during this time that my mom got me into the Big Brother program. My Big Brother was a doctor, a psychologist. He took a special interest in mentoring me and would visit on the weekend. We talked a lot, went on drives, and visited places I'd never seen. His visits were special because I didn't have a dad, at least not one that cared enough to visit. It really meant a lot to me to have him as a Big Brother. I've always wanted to tell him that.

Did you read a lot when you were a child?

You bet I did. We couldn't afford to buy books but that didn't stop me from reading. I remember going to the library with my mom. We'd go at least once a week and I could pick out any books I wanted. I thought I was the luckiest kid in the world. I didn't know or care that we were poor.

I remember being fascinated with the *Ripley's Believe It Or Not* books and *Guinness Book of World Records*. I loved the fantastic stories of people who could do incredible things, like swallowing swords or walking on fire.

I wasn't your typical young reader. I don't remember ever reading picture books. I do remember the librarians helping me find new books to read. They got me reading a lot of the classics—classics I still love like *Treasure Island*, *The Swiss Family Robinson*, *Kidnapped*, *Robinson Crusoe*, and *The Three Musketeers*.

I remember getting absolutely hooked on Jules Verne. I read *Around the World in Eighty Days*, *Twenty Thousand Leagues under the Sea*, and *Journey to the Center of the Earth*. I remember when *Journey to the Center of the Earth* came to the movies. I begged my mom for money so my little sister and I could go see it. We watched the movie three times that day. The only reason we left is because someone finally noticed these two kids who weren't leaving the theatre when the movie ended. Back then they didn't really check the theatres like they do now.

I also went through a Sherlock Holmes phase. I read every Sir Arthur Conan Doyle book I could find in the library. Those books led me to Edgar Rice Burroughs, but I'm not quite sure why now. I do remember reading the Tarzan books over and over, and it was through Burroughs that I discovered science fiction. His *The Martian Tales* series got me hooked on the genre. I went on to read Ray Bradbury's *The Martian Chronicles* and liked it so much I read

The Illustrated Man, Something Wicked This Way Comes, and *Fahrenheit 451.*

These are all books I read before my 10th birthday, so yes, I really did read a lot and I loved to read more than anything else.

Did you want to be a writer back then?

I'm not sure if I ever wanted to be a writer when I was younger. I did have a lot of influences leading me in that direction, though. I had a relative who worked for Golden Books in Racine. I think he used to give us kids activity and coloring books on birthdays and holidays.

In grade school I wrote for the school newspaper, and by the fourth grade I was a Junior Editor. I wrote several weekly columns, including the school sports column. I remember writing stories, but I think the earliest things I wrote were jokes and riddles. When I was 5 or 6 I thought they were funny, but looking back I don't think they were that funny.

I kept a journal back then and that's where I wrote down my stories and jokes. I would also paste in my columns from the school newspaper.

I was always fascinated by the lives of the writers whose stories I read. I always wanted to know how they lived, what they did, what life was like when they were alive, why they wrote. I would look up their biographies in the Encyclopedia Britannica. I remember getting a card game one year for Christmas that had to do with famous authors. It showed pictures of the authors, listed a brief biography. I played that game a lot and studied the cards. To me, those cards were better than baseball cards.

Did you have any pets when you were little?

In the city, we had a dog named Lobo. He was a Siberian husky. He helped watch the house and keep us kids safe. He had two different colored eyes. He was a great dog. In the winter he would pull us around in a sled. Since he was such a big dog, he usually stayed outside. He had a big thick chain attached to a spike in the ground and I always felt sorry for him when it was cold out. The dog next door would always bark at him, and one day Lobo broke his chain, jumped the fence, and killed the dog. It was a Great Dane and the owner was so mad he made us put Lobo down. I was heartbroken for a long time.

I got a tomcat after that. He was a cute kitten and grew to be huge. I've never seen a cat that big since. He liked to sneak out and roam the neighborhood. He would get in fights and sometimes wouldn't come home for days. Before we moved to the country, he got out. We'd go back to the old house to check for him hoping he'd be there but he never was. I never saw him again after that.

And we had another dog, Toby, who was around until after I went to the military. We also had other cats. One of the cats lived over 20 years and my mother kept her after all us kids moved out.

Tell us about your father and mother.

My father was a Hungarian immigrant. He came to America after the Hungarian Uprising in 1956. He fought to keep the communists out of Hungary and was sent to a Prisoner of War camp in Yugoslavia after Budapest fell to the communists. He escaped from the Prisoner of War camp and made his way to America where he hoped to start over. Part of his story appeared in an issue of Life Magazine.

When he arrived in New York, he found work at the J. I. Case tractor factory. Some years later he worked construction and later started his own construction company. He was a hard worker, but also haunted by what he'd seen growing up in Hungary during World War II and fighting during the Hungarian Uprising. I think that's why he drank so heavily.

My mother was the granddaughter of Norwegian and French immigrants who came to America with their parents. She, like my father, was a hard worker, but the two were never happy together. After they divorced, my mother raised us five kids by herself. That was hard for her, and for us. To make ends meet, she was always working. She worked a minimum-wage day job, and cleaned houses in the evenings and often on weekends. She tried not to show how tired she was after coming home from 12 to 16 hour days, but she was always tired.

Whenever my mom lost a job, things got tough. My grandparents could only help out so much and my mom didn't want to go on welfare except as a last resort, which it sometimes was. I remember weeks at a time where we ate nothing but flour and water pancakes at home. If it weren't for school lunches, I don't know what we would have done; but I don't regret growing up poor, my childhood or anything.

I learned a lot of life lessons early: the value of hard work, the value of money, the value of close family. My mother always made sure it was a happy house. The holidays were big at our house. Thanksgiving, Christmas, New Years were all big to-do's even if the food and the gifts were donations from the Salvation Army.

Did you always do as you were told?

Everyone makes mistakes. I wasn't perfect. Growing up in a rough neighborhood, I wasn't what you'd call an angel. I had to be smarter and faster than the bullies. If I wasn't fast enough, I had to fight or give up my lunch money or whatever else they wanted.

One time, it was the family groceries I was carrying back from the corner store, and that hurt a lot because we didn't have money to replace what was stolen and I knew that. I started stealing things after that. I don't know why, but I imagine it had something to do with trying to get even for what had happened.

When I was visiting friends of my mom's I got caught shoplifting, but I still hadn't learned my lesson. Later that same day, I stole some money from them and got caught again. I wasn't a very good thief, and it's a good thing. It was pure agony, and then getting caught—not once but twice—I learned my lesson quick.

Needless to say, my mom's friends didn't want us kids at their house after that—and me in particular.

Tell us about your grandparents.

My grandparents were a huge influence on my life. After the stealing incidents, some parents might have wanted to ship me off to military school. I was only 7 or 8 at the time, and while I might have been threatened with it, my grandparents thought of a better solution. They started sending us kids to Christian Bible Camp.

I think I went for the first time the year I was caught stealing, so I thought it was supposed to be a punishment. You know, send that darn kid away to find God and maybe he'll notice one of the Ten Commandments has to do with stealing.

The camp was called Camp Timber Lee. It was located in the heart of Wisconsin's farm country. I remember that kids of different age groups went at different times. My little sister cried and cried at summer camp. She was homesick every day. She wanted to go home.

When it came my turn to go, I was petrified. I didn't know what to expect, but when I got there I found out they had all these activities you could do. You could learn about nature, go on hikes, make arts and crafts, take archery lessons, go swimming, go sailing. And oh yeah, you couldn't skip certain things, like the bible lessons or the nighttime gatherings.

To my surprise, I loved camp and the best part about it was the nighttime gatherings where everyone got together to sing and learn about the bible. The next summer I hoped I could go again, but my grandparents paid for my cousins to go.

Fate was on my side though. My cousins hated camp, and as I was the only one who liked it, I got to go every summer after that.

The funny thing is that Camp Timber Lee really did change my outlook on life. I learned so much there. I learned how to swim, how to sail, how to kayak. I learned how to survive in nature. I also learned important lessons about values, morals, truth, and friendship. I made lifelong friends at camp. I even met my first girlfriend there.

My one regret about those summers is that I never did learn how to ride horses. Horseback riding was something that cost extra and I never did get up the courage to ask my grandparents if they'd pay for the lessons. It was enough that they were already paying for me to go to camp.

So now whenever I think of my grandparents, I think of Camp Timber Lee and all the things I learned and experienced there. Looking back, I'm sure going away from home every summer is what gave me the courage to leave home when it came time—and that was a good thing. It was the first, necessary step to becoming a best-selling writer.

Why did you move to the country?

My mom wanted us kids to have a normal life and she worked really hard to make sure we had as normal a life as we could. With my older sisters out of the house and just me and my little sister at home, she was afraid to leave us alone when she had to work at night or on the weekend. I could get into a lot of mischief in a few hours and so could my sister. Add to that the attempted burglary of our home—our dog Toby bit the gun-toting burglar on the butt—and I think my mom was more than ready to get out of the city.

The opportunity came when she found a farmhouse that hadn't been rented out in a while. The farmhouse was old, drafty, and required a lot of upkeep. But my mom didn't care about that. It was perfect, and she made sure it was perfect for us.

I still remember that yard. It was huge and had to be tended to—and we couldn't afford a fancy mower. We actually used a push mower—the kind powered by you pushing rather than an engine—to mow the lawn. I learned a lot about the value of hard work, following a schedule, and persistence helping to mow that lawn.

That lawn was something that had to be tended to every week or otherwise it was almost impossible to mow the next week. And it took hours and hours to finish, so we usually couldn't finish it all in a day. Instead, we spread out the mowing over several days.

Tell us about the farmhouse and growing up in the country.

The house was an old 2-story farmhouse on several acres of land. The long gravel drive that ran for several hundred yards from the road is the first thing I remember seeing. After that I remember going out into the yard. The yard had an apple tree, a cherry tree, a few oak trees, a big hill, and a sunken area that as a kid I imagined was a valley.

The house was just at the start of a small lakeside community and we were within walking distance of the lake. In the summer, my sister and I would spend all day walking around the lake, chasing frogs and fish. There was a store on one side of the lake where we'd go buy soda pop and snacks if we found some change.

In the other direction, there were farm fields. A stream ran through the fields and we'd follow it endlessly when the weather was warm. We'd pretend to be adventurers. If you followed the stream for a few miles, there was a dump that had been used by farmers a long time ago.

We found a lot of cool stuff there. Mostly old beer cans and bottles, but the stuff was fifty years old so we thought it was treasure. If you walked another few miles, you ended up in a small town, and we sometimes stopped in the general store there; or we'd go over by the mushroom farm and watch the horses run in the fields.

In the fall we'd build giant leaf piles and jump into them. One time I burrowed into the hill under the leaf pile, thinking I was something of a hobbit. It was the same time that the badgers moved into the brush down the hill—so digging a huge, inviting hole wasn't a good idea as I later found out.

In the winter, we'd build these huge snow forts. We'd add to the snow fort as long as the snow and cold weather lasted. Sometimes we'd end up with a dozen tunnels and rooms, all under the snow.

What else do you remember about living there?

Well, living in the country wasn't all peaches and cream. We had neighborhood bullies there too. One in particular picked on my sister and me every day, at least until I decided I had had enough. He tried to pick on me in the schoolyard and I got up just enough courage to stand up to him. I think he won the fight, because I ended up with him sitting on me, pummeling me, but he got the black eye and never bothered me again after that.

I remember also that the bus rides from school were incredibly long. On the way to school, we were the last to be picked up, so we went straight to school, but on the way home we were the last to get off the bus. We went out deep into farm country before going back to where I lived and that took over an hour, sometimes an hour and a half.

Long bus rides like that were boring. I read a lot to pass the time.

What was it like not having your father in your life?

Not having a father in my life was painful. It was lonely sometimes. He rarely called or visited. It was as though us kids just weren't a part of his life that was important. To make things worse, he never paid child support.

The only time he ever sent us anything or bought us anything was at Christmas. When I was older he'd sometimes send a few hundred dollars through Western Union. That was it, and let me tell you a few hundred dollars didn't go far.

I have few memories of visiting my father when he lived in Wisconsin with his second wife. The first time I clearly remember visiting him is when I was 10 or 12. My mom, my younger sister, and I took a trip to Mississippi, where he lived at that time. It was a fun trip. He bought us clothes, took us out fishing on his boat. We went out to eat a lot and I remember a big barbeque.

That trip was one of the happiest and one of the saddest times of my life. I was happy because the Gulf Coast is a beautiful place to visit and because I was with my father. I was sad because it was the first time that I realized my father was wealthy. He was running a construction business in Mississippi and Texas. He had 3 houses, a 40' boat, cars, trucks, all kinds of expensive things. On the other side of that was my mom and us kids struggling to make ends meet, struggling just to get by.

I wondered if he'd care that I spent my free time mowing lawns and doing odd jobs just to help make ends meet. Somehow I didn't think he would, and that made me very sad.

After that trip, I'd visit sometimes in the summer. I remember visiting when I was 15 or 16, then again when I was 17.

School Days

Tell me about your first school.

My first school was Janes School Elementary in Racine, Wisconsin. Janes School is in a turn-of-the-century schoolhouse.

The main section was built in the late 1800's and is the same school that my grandfather attended for several years during his primary school days. In the early 1900's there were two schools running out of the same building: one on the first floor and another on the second floor. My grandfather went to the school on the second floor.

I loved that old school. It had oak floors and the lower level was split into several sections. You went down one set of stairs to go to the gym and cafeteria, then after lunch we'd go up a different set of stairs to go out into the schoolyard.

As a kindergartner, I remember being afraid of all those stairs but they were fun once I learned how to navigate them.

My first teacher was very strict. It was a public school, but she had a lot of rules of her own that were probably carried over from her days in private schools.

One of those rules was that children shouldn't write with their left hand. Bad children wrote with their left hand. Good children wrote with their right hand. At least that's how it was in her day and in her mind.

I remember getting whacked on the knuckles every time I tried to color or draw with my left hand. I came home with a swollen hand one day and couldn't move my fingers. My mom walked me right back to school and had it out with the teacher. The teacher never whacked me with a ruler again. I'm still left-handed by the way.

Teacher's Classroom Guide: An Interview with Robert Stanek

Tell me about your walks to school.

I really loved walking to school. I remember the whole walk—it was about 4 blocks—but it seemed like miles back then. Everything seems so big or long when you're small. We lived in a tough neighborhood so I didn't walk alone much, but sometimes I did and I was really scared.

A few years ago I went back to Racine and visited the neighborhood where I grew up. The green, 2-story house was still there. It looked exactly like it did when I lived there. I also drove along the route I used to take to school. I couldn't believe it was only a few blocks—I still had this memory of how long the walk was and how far away the school was.

I was delighted to find that the old school was still there too. I went in and visited, surprised at all the memories that the visit brought back. Despite the ruler-whacking incident, I really loved that school. All my teachers after kindergarten were wonderful and I attended Janes School until the fourth grade. After that, we moved to the country and I attended Wheaton Elementary.

What do you remember about that school?

Wheaton Elementary was different than I expected. In the city, the next year I would have been in 5th grade and been one of the big kids in the schoolyard, and being big or small made a huge difference as you know from my comments about bullies. I was also the older brother taking my younger sister to school, so I felt like I had a tremendous amount of responsibility.

When we moved, I found out the new school went from Kindergarten to 8th grade and instead of walking we rode the school bus. So not only was I not one of the big kids any more, I also didn't have any big brother responsibilities. I had looked forward to being the big brother for a change.

I soon found out that was the least of my worries. I had no friends at the new school. I didn't know anyone and it was my bad luck to get seated within spitting distance from the class bully. I went from being one of the happiest, most attentive kids to being one of the most miserable.

I hated school for a while after that. I went from being very outgoing to being someone who rarely said anything. I didn't want to go to school sometimes. I'd beg to stay home. My mom would let me sometimes.

I hid in my books for a long time. But it wasn't all bad. The school had a great library. It was easily twice the size as the library at my old school.

That year I discovered Herman Melville, Jack London, Charles Dickens, and Edgar Allan Poe. Edgar Allan Poe can be pretty bleak and dark, especially when you're ten years old. But I remember being fascinated with his stories. To this day, I can still remember parts of *The Raven*, *The Tell Tale Heart*, and *The Murders in the Rue Morgue*.

Those books and stories became like friends, so it made things a lot better. I did eventually make friends and I started liking school again, so that made things better too.

Tell us about moving and changing schools.

I've probably moved more than anyone you'll ever know. Being in the military, I had to move around a lot with my own family as well. My son asked me one time how many times I moved in my life. I stopped to think about it and it took about ten minutes to figure out. I counted eighteen moves—seven of those when I was a kid. Personally, I think there's some Hungarian gypsy blood in me, but can't confirm it.

Back to that move, that time we moved closer to the city because my mom got a new job in the sheriff's department. The timing was awful. We moved partway through my freshman year of high school (9th grade).

High School was different from grade school. In our area kids for all over the county attended one of two high schools, so kids from many different grade schools attended each. It was a big adjustment for me because the school was terrifyingly huge. Then just when I made a bunch of new friends and learned how to get around the school, we moved.

I went from Wilmot High School to Central High School. Because the schools zones weren't that far apart, some of the kids from my old school went there, but none of them were my friends. Basically I had to start all over: make new friends, learn how to get around the school, all of it.

Moving a lot as a child was really awful and it was lonely a lot of the time, but I met a lot more people and was exposed to much more than the average kid. I learned a lot about people and myself because of all those moves. I had a lot of great teachers along the way.

In the end, I think all those moves better prepared me for life. I know people that are scared to death of moving. They don't want to leave the area they grew up. They don't want things to change. They want everything just as it was.

Teacher's Classroom Guide: An Interview with Robert Stanek

The problem with that is that things do change. You have to adapt and move on. If you don't you may get stuck living in the past where the best time of your life is your school days and not the present where you should be happy and fulfilled.

My younger sister is a perfect example of that. I think all those moves made her more resistant to change. After graduation she stayed in the same small town for the next 20 years, worked minimum-wage jobs, barely got by.

A few years ago she and her husband decided to make a positive change in their life. Their church was a big influence in the decision and I'm thankful for that.

They moved with their family to a place where they could both make a living wage and had opportunities to grow their skills. So far so good, they now enjoy a comfortable life and have money to take vacations and travel.

Who was your favorite teacher?

With all those moves and new schools, I had many favorite teachers. The teachers I remember clearest in my memory are my high school teachers. I was always a strong student, even when I was a bit rebellious, so I was in the advanced and honors classes. You know, honors English all that.

In the sciences, I took biology, chemistry and physics. My biology/physics teacher was a lot of fun. He was a bit portly and had a beard. He would tell jokes and do silly things that just made learning fun. Our school was one of the first to get computers—remember, I went to high school in the 80's and computers were just starting to be available for home and school use.

We had Apple II's and the same teacher was in that class too. It was on the honor system, so you just went to the computer lab and did whatever as long as you turned in the assignments.

Computers opened up a whole new world for me. By the end of the year, I was programming game code in binary and assembly. I made a game called Beer Wars where you had to blast pretzels, beer kegs, and beer bottles—you can probably tell I was going through a bit of a rebellious stage then.

With computers, I was hooked right from the start.

Another teacher that was a big influence on me was my mathematics teacher. I advanced in math through calculus in high school. My calculus teacher was a brilliant man. Problem is

Teacher's Classroom Guide: An Interview with Robert Stanek

I had his class first thing in the morning. At that time, I was running with the wrong crowd of kids, doing things at all hours of the night that I shouldn't have been doing.

I would always get to his class late. I'd have to stop off in the bathroom too because I had these wicked allergies. I never had allergies before so I didn't know what to do. My nose was always running. If I were going to school today, the teachers probably would've thought I was on drugs but I wasn't into those types of things.

Drugs are bad for you. They'll mess you up for life. I knew better than to use drugs. One of my sisters had smoked marijuana and I remember what happened when my mom found out.

I didn't know about alcohol though. My father was an alcoholic, so I thought drinking was okay. Even at a young age, I remember visiting my father sometimes and stealing beer when he wasn't watching. I'd run off with his wife's kids from his second marriage and go drink it. So when I got older, I thought it was okay to drink too. But drinking can be as bad as drugs. It was screwing up my life.

Anyway this teacher was a big help. I think he knew I was screwing up and may have suspected what I was doing. He didn't punish me or turn me in though. I had an A+ average in his class, never missed a point, so I think that was part of it. It was the one time in my life I ever got special treatment for being smart and it helped.

Another teacher that was a big influence on me was my typing teacher, believe it or not. She was the greatest. At that time, we worked on a mix of electric and manual typewriters. I was one of the only boys in a class full of girls. The only boy in Typing II, when I took a second semester, that's for sure.

People thought this honors student was taking typing to goof off. But that wasn't it at all. When I started programming computers, I recognized immediately how important being able to type was to programming and if there was ever a better typing teacher, I've never met one.

By the end of that second semester, I was typing 60 words a minute. We learned business skills in those classes too. Those skills have helped me in every job I've ever held. And I don't think I'd be a writer if I didn't know how to type. I'd be too frustrated.

Teacher's Classroom Guide: An Interview with Robert Stanek

Was there anything you didn't like about school?

Well that's a funny question. Isn't it?

I didn't always like school. I did have some teachers that were mean. I remember clearly an English teacher who gave me an F on a test that was a third of the grade, which gave me a D+ for the semester. She said I didn't follow directions, but I did. She was a bully of the worst sort and it's easy for teachers to use their authority to be bullies.

I don't think she liked this poor kid with ragged clothes in her honors class. Our house had burned down that year, so I was wearing had-me-downs from the Salvation Army and Goodwill. I didn't fit in with the other kids and their middle-class backgrounds.

That teacher should have been the one to help me the most because she was in a position to. She helped other kids. Instead of helping me, she made sure my grade point average didn't threaten any of her stars.

People who think being smart is a ticket to success don't understand life. There are a lot of smart people who never get a chance.

That incident taught me one of the great truths of my life. I already knew other kids disliked brainiac/nerd types, but that was my first experience with an adult, someone I looked up to. It was like a wake up call to force myself to be genuinely average, to coast by, to not stand out, to not get noticed. That's how much of an impact that incident had on my life.

Staggering success as an underachiever is overrated though. You get nowhere, become nothing. All through my school days I would've traded brains for brawn any time. The jocks, the school athletes, were the ones teachers rewarded and all the kids liked.

But what I discovered much later in life changed my viewpoint on that. What I discovered is that some people will feel threatened if you are smart. Some people will dislike you because you are smart. They might not hire you. They might not promote you. They might try to discredit you. You may get a new boss of this type who may fire you or make you so miserable you quit.

I've found this to be true in the military, in Fortune 500 companies, in small business. It's sad but it's true everywhere. I've found few exceptions.

Truth is though, if you work hard and are willing to stand up for yourself, you can make it. You can achieve your dreams.

Never give up.

When you make it, do me a favor. Look back fondly on your past. Forget about all those people who tried to hold you back, who put you down, who made you feel unimportant.

Remember instead the ones who helped. Remember instead that adversity made you stronger, better. Remember that there are people who understand what you're going through, what you went through. The world isn't a perfect place, but for each and every one of us, it is what we decide to make it.

Outside of school, what was your childhood like?

I don't think there are a lot of people who have a childhood like mine. I knew at a young age that my life was anything but charmed. There was a lot of tragedy in my life. That tragedy shaped who I was then and who I am today.

When I was very young my mom remarried. He was a former navy enlisted man. They were truly in love. They bought a house in Sturtevant, Wisconsin. Shortly afterward, my younger sister was born. It was a very happy time, but all too short, like most such times in my life.

One day, my step-dad went to down to the basement to check the gas hot-water heater because we had no hot water. A repairman had been out to fix the hot-water heater several times, but it never worked right. When my step-dad struck a match to relight the heater, the whole house exploded. The heater had been leaking gas and it was everywhere.

He was engulfed in flames and was burned over 80 percent of his body. My sister, Bridgette, who had been standing behind him, was knocked out the basement door by the blast.

She was rushed to the hospital with my step-dad. The hospital was very busy that day. My step-dad was rushed away to a burn unit, where he died a few days later.

All us kids waited in the emergency room with my mom. My mom kept asking the nurse to look at my sister, but no one ever did. A few hours later, Bridgette just closed her eyes and never woke up again. She had a brain injury—something doctors and nurses now know to look for after that type of trauma, but I don't think they did back then.

I remember crying for days. It was a sad time. It was right after that that we moved to the green 2-story house in Racine.

Teacher's Classroom Guide: An Interview with Robert Stanek

Have you ever gone back to the schools you attended?

I did actually. Being in the military kept me away from Wisconsin for a long time, and it was 20 years before I made an extended visit and had time to travel around a bit.

I visited Janes School Elementary first, surprised at how many memories that brought back. I hadn't been in the old schoolhouse for all those years, but I remembered it. I remembered my first grade classroom, the halls, all those stairs that made the school seem like a labyrinth. I remembered the cafeteria and the gym, and the schoolyard where I pitched marbles.

Visiting my other schools brought a flood of memories too.

Did you really get leaches all over you one time?

I did. When we moved to the farmhouse, there was that stream nearby. We'd go there and play all the time. The streambed was real muddy, and a lot of time as we followed the stream we'd slosh in the water. Sometimes in our bare feet, sometimes with our tennis shoes on.

We knew the stream had leaches because most of the time if you stepped too deep in the mud you'd take your foot out and find leaches. Eek!

You could pinch them and pull them off. If you were fast, they wouldn't have a chance to get a good hold of your flesh, but a lot of the time you had to rip them off and that hurt.

One time, I was trying to cross the stream, walking on top of a row of rocks. The rocks were slippery and wet from my sister sloshing across just before me. I never made it across. I fell on my backside into the water. With the water running fast from the spring runoff, it took my some time to get out. I got stuck in the muck on the far bank too.

I felt them crawling on me right away. By the time I ripped my shirt off, I knew they were everywhere. I had to take off my shoes, my socks, my pants.

My sister helped me start pulling all the leaches off. They were on my back, legs, between my toes, under my arms. I was just happy they didn't manage to get someplace else, though. You know where.

Oh!, that would have been painful. It's painful even thinking about it now.

Did you watch a lot of television?

Well, we didn't have cable TV back then, so there really wasn't much to watch. I know some parts of the city did. I remember my grandpa had cable. We didn't. We used a rabbit ears antenna on top of the TV.

We were lucky to be close to Chicago and Milwaukee though, so we got some channels. I remember watching WGN out of Chicago the most. It played a lot of oldies and I liked the black and white shows the best.

I'd watch The Three Stooges, Gilligan's Island, Mr. Ed, Superman. I remember getting up at 5 a.m. to watch Topper and The Lone Ranger. I liked the old Abbott and Costello movies, too.

On the weekend, they had Creature Theatre. I'd watch Dracula, Frankenstein, Godzilla, the Mummy, that kind of stuff. But I really didn't watch that much TV.

Instead of watching TV, I read or listened to old radio programming. I had a whole collection of oldies on tape. The Green Hornet, War of the Worlds, The Lone Ranger again—I liked stories with clear heroes and villains.

Do you miss those times?

For me it really was the best of times and the worst of times. I do miss it sometimes.

It wasn't all sugar and gumdrops, but it's what I had. Like I said, my mom always worked hard to make sure we had as happy a home as possible. That was huge for me.

Every kid needs one person who loves them that much. A dad, a mom, a brother, a sister, an uncle, an aunt, a teacher, whatever. It really does make all the difference. If you don't have that kind of support, there are places to find it. The Boy Scouts and Girls Scouts of America, Big Brothers Big Sisters, the YMCA to name a few.

My mom knew she couldn't do it all. She sowed the seeds, got us interested in things: museums, libraries, Boy Scouts, Girl Scouts, church. Then she let us decide what we wanted to do.

One year, you know, the one where I was caught stealing, she started sending us kids to Sunday school. Between Christian Bible Camp in the summer and Christian Bible School on Sundays, I got the message and mended my ways pretty darn quick.

After that, Sunday school became optional. Go if you want to.

My sister and I did go for a few more years.

Teacher's Classroom Guide: An Interview with Robert Stanek

A car hit you when you were young. What happened?

Sometimes I feel like my childhood was a car wreck, but that one happened when I was in the 5th grade. It was the year after we moved to the farmhouse. I went out for a ride on a new bike. A gift from my Big Brother to replace the bike that had been stolen in the city.

I rode down the hill from our house, went around the corner. I remember looking down a stretch of straight road and then wham! the car hit me from behind. The driver was going really fast and the car slammed into the bike like it wasn't there. The bike ended up with the back tire twisted around all the way to where the front tire used to be, before it broke off the frame. I flew off the bike and landed on the pavement. The car drove over the bike and stopped just after it drove over me and started to drag me down the road.

The driver was a drunken school teacher. She picked me up off the road, put my bike in the trunk of her car, and then drove to her house. I was unconscious so I don't remember exactly, but I know she never called for an ambulance.

She called her husband, waited till she sobered up. It must have taken a few hours because by the time my mom came and got me it was dark out, and I had gone out for the ride early in the afternoon.

I was conscious then, barely, scraped and bruised from head to toe. My clothes were all torn up, shredded like I'd been dragged behind the car. But I didn't have any broken bones.

The school teacher told my mom she'd hit me with her car and I'd scraped my knee, could she come and get me. I remember my mom screaming and screaming when she saw me. It was the school teacher's husband or her son who carried me out to my mom's car. Afterward, I remember he put my broken up bike in the back of my mom's station wagon and then they pretty much closed the door in my mom's face.

I missed a few weeks of school, recovering in a chair next to the TV. It was a miserable time because I hurt everywhere and the pain was intense whenever I moved. We couldn't afford a hospital, so I stayed in that chair till I got better. I don't remember ever visiting a doctor either.

The school teacher never checked to see how I was doing. An insurance adjuster showed up a few weeks later. He convinced my mom that $500 and a new bike was worth signing a paper saying that we weren't going to sue.

Military Career

Why did you join the military?

That's the $64,000 question, isn't it? I've been asked that a lot. Smart kid should have gotten a scholarship, gone to a good school. But that's not how it worked out.

I didn't know how to apply for scholarships, loans, or grants. I had no idea where to begin. There was no one there to help. No one in my family had ever gone to college so no one knew how that stuff worked. My mom was always working.

At school, teachers that maybe should have helped focused on other kids—you know the ones with parents who could afford to pay for college, or most of it—and the school programs were all about preparing for the SAT or taking the AFQT (Armed Forces Qualifying Test). They didn't teach us anything about what we needed to do to get into college.

I took the SAT because it got me out of school for a day. My scores were respectable for someone who never prepared for the exam or cared about the score. I would have had my choice of several colleges if I had applied. But who was going to pay for it?

I took the AFQT because they gave it in school—during school. My high score meant about as much as my SAT score—nothing, at least to me. Recruiters loved it though, and I had a sister that was already in the Air Force, so the Air Force recruiter was particularly persistent.

As my high school graduation day approached, I had no idea what I was going to do with my life. To complicate matters, my mom had just remarried. She moved with her new husband and my sister to northern Wisconsin a few months before graduation. I stayed with a friend so I could finish out the school year and go to graduation.

Teacher's Classroom Guide: An Interview with Robert Stanek

After graduation I visited my dad in Mississippi. I had worked for him before in the summer, doing roofing and siding. It paid well, but the hours were long. Most of the summer we'd work sunup till sundown, and let me tell you, there are few places hotter than the side of a building or a roof in the summer.

I already knew construction was something I didn't want to do for a living, but I went anyway. It gave me a destination, a place to go.

I mentioned to my dad that I wanted to go to college. He got me interested in an aeronautical engineering school in Florida. He had been a pilot in the Hungarian Air Force. We visited the school, but I knew right away that my father had no intention of paying for it.

Instead, he wanted me to join the Air Force so I could fly planes like he did. The only problem was that he didn't understand that I'd never be a pilot without a college degree. He didn't need a degree to fly, so why would I? But that's the way it is in the U.S. military.

We visited the Air Force recruiter that same week. I took the ASVAB (Armed Services Vocational Aptitude and Battery Test) a few days later. With my scores, the recruiter told me I could enlist and get any specialty I wanted. He even told my dad that I could become an aircraft mechanic and get stationed right there in Mississippi.

My dad loved that idea. I didn't so much, so after the summer I went back to Wisconsin. My mom was living in northern Wisconsin, so that's where I went.

By the holidays I was completely miserable. I didn't know many people. I didn't have a job. I knew my life was going nowhere. I knew I needed to make a change or I'd be stuck going down a one-way street into a dead end.

I decided to go talk to the Air Force recruiter again. We talked a lot about the career fields that were available and where I'd fit in with my skills. The career field that got my interest was Intelligence, and the particular specialty of cryptologic linguist.

All the training associated with that career fascinated me. Weeks of intensive language school, weeks of analytics school, weeks of specialty training. Nearly 2 years of training in all. I thought it'd be like getting a degree only better—I'd have a sure job waiting at the end of it all.

I enlisted right then.

Teacher's Classroom Guide: An Interview with Robert Stanek

What do you remember about basic training?

The Air Force conducts basic training at Lackland Air Force Base in San Antonio, Texas. I flew from Milwaukee to New Orleans, and then the next day I took a military bus to San Antonio. That bus ride was the longest of my life. I knew basic training was at the end of it and I'll be the first to admit I was scared.

Someone should have told me from the start that basic training was a head game designed to break you down and rebuild you as a model soldier. As a thinker, I would have understood it a lot better. I got by, though.

The drill sergeants start by taking away your identity. They strip you of all your belongings—your ties to home and family. They shave men's hair, cut women's hair, then put everyone in a uniform. Every trainee should look like every other trainee. That's the thinking.

I was an ugly bald guy.

Drill teaches discipline. Classroom instruction teaches military rules and codes of conduct.

All the other stuff—ironing your clothes, polishing your boots, folding your bed sheets—is pretty much designed to teach conformity and uniformity. It also keeps your thoughts focused on basic training and helps you to forget about your life outside the military.

It worked pretty well too. I was frequently terrified. I graduated basic training with honors, a model soldier.

Was language school hard?

The first day of language school was a wake up call for me. I thought that since basic training was over life would go back to normal. That was hardly the case.

At that time, the Air Force trained linguists at Lackland Air Force Base and at Presidio of Monterrey, California. I thought I'd be going to California. I was ready to learn how to surf. Instead of going to California, though, I stayed in Texas—it seemed to be the start of 47 weeks of hell.

Language school at Lackland followed many of the same rules as basic training. We had daily inspections, drill, physical training (PT), marching—the whole enchilada. It really felt like an extended basic training. To make matters worse, my training instructor singled me out as the one he was going to wash out, i.e. force out of the program.

He tried for 47 weeks to fail me out of the training program. He'd fail my room on inspections—even if it was spotless. We had 35-10 (military uniform and appearance) inspection once a week, so I knew when it was coming. I'd get a hair cut the day before but he'd still fail me and make me go get another hair cut.

Sometimes he'd give surprise inspections and fail me for not shaving. But I shaved every day. In basic training I had to shave twice a day to keep up the appearance of a baby smooth face. That tears up your face after a while though, so I couldn't shave twice a day every day.

While failing inspections gave me extra duties and kept me from getting liberties a lot of the time, it didn't fail me out of the training program. To get thrown out of the program, I would have also had to be failing my classes.

No, the only thing his bullying did was to keep my stress level high. I think he wanted me to quit because you could voluntarily quit the program and they'd send you to perform other duties—the types of duties the Air Force couldn't normally fill. One of my friends quit the program and the Air Force sent him to clean snow off runways in Alaska for the rest of his enlistment.

In fact, the fear of getting sent to that kind of duty is what kept many of us going. I had enlisted for 4 years and on the first day of language training our unit commander invited all 65 of us new trainees to look around the room. I'll never forget what he said. He said don't count on the person standing next to you being there in 47 weeks. He said don't count on anyone getting you through this training but you. He said ten of us wouldn't be here in 2 weeks, and most of the rest of us would be gone before graduation.

He was right. Only 22 out of 65 made it to graduation. The kicker was that language training was only the beginning. Each graduate had months of additional training to look forward to.

Where did you go next?

I went to Goodfellow Air Force Base, Texas. I spent the next 20 weeks learning how to be an analyst. When people think of intelligence analysts they often think of Tom Clancy's Jack Ryan. Jack Ryan's a fictitious character. What we were training to do was real.

We trained in a vault-like building with high security everywhere. There were guards, wire fences, dogs, security systems. We had to have top-security clearances and badges to get into the building.

Analyst training was intense. Unlike language training we relied on each other a lot more to get through the days and weeks.

The training gave new meaning to the word stress. They worked us in rotating shifts to see if we could handle the rigor of changing schedules in addition to learning the job we would do in the field. Some people cracked under that pressure. They left the program because their grades slumped and they couldn't get back on track or because they simply were too tired of trying to make it through.

But for the most part, they didn't wash out because the instructors wanted them out. The instructors knew the value of training we'd already received. They'd move failing students back to a class that was just starting, give them a chance to start over, that kind of thing, if possible. Still, only 15 of the 22 from my original group graduated and went on to field duties.

Did you like living in Texas?

Despite the fact that the early days in language training were like basic training, it wasn't all that way. Eventually, I did get into what was called Phase 3, which allowed me to go off base after hours and on weekends.

I had an old black thunderbird, so I would cruise around San Antonio. When you are in such an intense environment, you make a lot of close friends. A group of us would go out on the town a lot. We'd go to the college bars uptown, the River Walk area, that kind of thing.

The Alamo is in San Antonio, so that was a fun visit. But the best time I ever had was tubing down the Guadeloupe River. Several classes of students went to the river that day. We rented these huge inner tubes and floated down the river all day.

Goodfellow is in San Angelo, Texas. It's a college town, so it had a great night scene and there was a lot to do on the weekends. Groups of us would go to a bar called O'Malley's. They had all you can eat specials several days a week. We spent a lot of time—and money—there.

The military had a great recreation area nearby with a lake. We'd rent boats, jet skis. Blow off a lot of steam.

Teacher's Classroom Guide: An Interview with Robert Stanek

Tell me about your first assignment.

Toward the end of training at Goodfellow AFB we had the chance to choose the bases we wanted to get stationed at. My top choice was Berlin, Germany. I wanted to be stationed right in the heart of East Germany. I wanted to see the Berlin Wall, plus I had heard that the base was in an old bunker complex. My second choice was Japan. I didn't know much about Japan at that time. I had heard it was beautiful and that there was a lot to see. My third choice was England. Being stationed in England would have been great.

The assignment I got was Japan. I'd be stationed at Misawa Air Base, Japan, attached to the Electronic Security Group. Five of the 15 in my group went to Japan in fact, but only one of those was someone I hung around with, so I was kind of sad. Then when we got to Japan, we all got assigned to different flights. There were Alpha, Bravo, Charlie, and Delta flights, plus a flight of day crew.

I was assigned to Charlie flight. It was late fall when I arrived in Japan, and over 18 months since I had joined the air force. The building we worked in was a huge complex next to an enormous array of communications towers and a massive antennae structure called the Elephant Cage.

The facility was unique in that all branches of the U.S. armed forces worked there. We had army, air force, navy, and marines.

My first day on duty was a mid shift, meaning I had to work from midnight to 8 a.m. Let me tell you, it wasn't a good way to start.

We worked this crazy 4-4-4-3 rotation, which meant we worked 4 days (8 a.m. to 4 p.m.) had 24 hours off, then worked 4 swings (4 p.m. to 12 a.m.), followed by 24-hours off and 4 mids (12 a.m. to 8 a.m.). At the end of the rotation, we got 72 hours off.

Supposedly, this was a good shift rotation to work. I didn't buy it. But it was better than what our navy counterparts were working. They worked what was called double-backs. They worked two 8-hour day shifts followed by a 16-hour day-swing shift, followed by 2 swing shifts, a 16-hour swing-mid shift and 2 mid shifts before getting 96 hours off duty.

Anyway, that's how I remember my new supervisor breaking the news to me, that we basically worked 12 days and then got 3 off. Her "It could be worse" explanation worked pretty well. In fact, any time I felt worn out by the schedule, I remembered that and was thankful I didn't work the grinding 10-day crammed into 8 days rotation that the navy worked.

Teacher's Classroom Guide: An Interview with Robert Stanek

Did training end once you got to your first assignment?

No. Right after my supervisor explained the rotating shift I'd be working she set down this huge pile of binders next to me. Then she began explaining that I had 12-weeks to learn everything that the binders contained. At that point, I remembered thinking "Or what?" What were they going to do to me if I just didn't want to learn any more? Wasn't all that training I had had supposed to prepare me for my first assignment?

Turned out that all the training was just leading up to the first assignment, providing the foundation as it were. In the field, each station had its own training regimen that was specific to the duties at that station, and the set of binders in front of me was just for one area of specialty. If I wanted to go into other specialty areas, I'd have to go through training for those specialties too.

She set a challenge before me, though. I felt compelled to accept. I loved being an Intelligence Analyst. She knew it too, from my prior training and grades. From the first day, we both knew I was a natural and by the second day, I was already working alone—something that took most new personnel several weeks.

I learned the material in 4 weeks, took and passed the exams with one of the highest scores they'd ever scene. I went into another specialty that would move me from direct operations to more intense field analysis. That training was supposed to last 12 weeks too, but I finished it in three.

By Christmas this fresh-from-training airman, me, was running the line analysis. I was telling Staff Sergeants and up what to do and when to do it. Let me tell you, that didn't go over too well and ruffled a few feathers.

But that's how it was. There was a chain of command and a rank structure, but if you were the best at the job, you determined what happened when and how things were done. It was a good thing that I had learned from past mistakes and knew better than to let it go to my head. I knew I walked a fine line. I didn't abuse the privilege.

Still, I lived and breathed that stuff. I received three more certifications, including one that was reserved only for the most advanced experts at that assignment. I liked the duty so much that at the end of the second year, I extended for another year.

Teacher's Classroom Guide: An Interview with Robert Stanek

Did you travel in Japan?

Japan is a wonderful, beautiful country. Back then I belonged to the school of work hard, play hard. I was in the Orient, the Far East. I wasn't about to let that opportunity pass me by.

Japan is an island nation with four large islands and many small islands. Honshû is the largest island and I was stationed in northern Honshû in the Tôhoku region. The area to the north of us was mountainous. I loved being able to visit the mountains and the ocean all in the same day.

On break I spent more time off base than on base. I traveled all over. On the Japanese island of Hokkaidô in Sapporo they have these wonderful Ice Festivals. The ice sculptures are amazing. I've never seen anything like it since.

In the spring, the Japanese celebrate the Cherry Blossom Festival. I'd go every year to a city in the northeast where they had these ancient temples and you could go walk around the grounds during the festival.

I'd take day trips to Aomori all the time. I liked that city. There was a lot to see and do and it was far enough away from the base that the people were very open and friendly.

My favorite trips were to Tokyo. Tokyo is in the Kantô region of Honshû so I could drive there. The road tolls were high though. Round trip it cost a few hundred dollars to drive and it was expensive to stay there, so I only went a few times, but I had a blast when I was there.

Did you learn Japanese?

I took Japanese classes and studied on my own as well. Spending a lot of time off base helped too. I had several friends who were Japanese. They'd help me with Japanese, and I'd help them with English.

I was particularly smitten with a Japanese girl for a while, so that made me want to learn Japanese in a hurry so we could communicate. She was my first true love, but her family didn't want her to get so deeply involved with an American. We dated for a while and she came to see me when I left Japan, but we both knew it could be nothing more than it was.

Did you study martial arts?

I took kendo lessons, the Japanese art of fencing. I had the privilege of studying in one of the local martial arts training schools. At first, they weren't going to admit me. There weren't any other Americans training at the school, but I persisted.

I attended the sessions, watched the students training, learned as much as I could from watching. Finally, one day, the master presented me with my own kendo sword.

In Japan, martial arts are so much a part of the culture—like hotdogs, baseball, and apple pie are in the U.S. Japanese don't just take martial arts lessons. Martial arts are a part of who they are.

For many Japanese, it's not a question of whether they are going to learn martial arts, but what disciplines they are going to master. At least that's how it was explained to me, and for me it was a great honor and a privilege to be able to take lessons.

At my skill level though, I couldn't train with the adults. I had to train with the children. It was tough getting beaten by 9 and 10 year olds who had already been practicing kendo for many years. Most students start training at 4 or 5. I learned humility in a hurry.

When I left Japan, I regretted that I hadn't started lessons earlier.

Where did you go after Japan?

In Japan I learned a lot about myself and what I could do as an Intelligence Analyst. One of my supervisors told me that I'd be a perfect candidate for airborne duty. Flying on secretive missions seemed extraordinarily appealing. I didn't give much thought to the fact that I could die doing that type of duty. Before my next assignment, I volunteered and was accepted into the airborne training program.

The first step in airborne training was survival school. After that I went to air combat school, then to a new assignment in Germany as a member of the combat crew flying on electronic warfare aircraft.

Was survival school really scary?

Survival school was one of the most exhilarating and challenging experiences of my life up until that time—and yes, it was a truly frightening experience at times. Training began with classroom instruction, then I went on to wilderness survival, prisoner of war training, and water survival training.

Teacher's Classroom Guide: An Interview with Robert Stanek

Survival school for the Air Force is conducted at Fairchild AFB, Washington. It was February when I went and bone cold in the mountains. I learned how to survive in the wilderness with nothing but the clothes on my back and a parachute. The same gear I'd have if a plane crash-landed somewhere and I had to parachute out of the plane.

I learned a lot: how to find food, what types of plants are edible, how to light a fire with flint and steal, how to get drinking water, how to find my way through the wilderness. That type of stuff.

The day after wilderness training, just when I would have had enough time to get a hot meal for the first time in weeks, they sent us on a bus ride. During that bus ride, "commandos" stormed the bus and took the entire team hostage. It seemed frightfully real at the time.

A black bag was put over my head, my hands were tied, and I was taken away with everyone else. The next thing I knew I was marching through a building and was then shoved into a tiny holding cell. I was alone in the dark.

The time was made worse by the music pouring out of the speakers. I'll never forget it. "Boot, boots, marching over Africa," the song went, and they played it over and over along with air raid sirens.

They kept me standing all through the night, hosed me down with cold water if I sat or fell asleep. The next morning they gave me dried oats and water. It was the only food served that day, and I had nothing the previous night.

I didn't eat and besides, before I could start, I was hauled away for "interrogation." The interrogators job was to break you down get you to say things. If you refused, you ended up in a box. I ended up in the box. The only way I could fit was to get into the fetal position. The box was dark and locked.

While I was in there, I could hear others screaming. One big guy just wouldn't fit in the box. I knew who he was by the sound of his voice. He was 6' 5", 250 pounds. They had to push and squeeze to get me into the box. I was 6' 2", 190 pounds at the time.

Another guy was claustrophobic. He was terrified of small places. He fought back, resisted.

It seemed we stayed in those boxes for hours.

To keep you from sleeping, they pounded on the boxes, just like they had pounded on our cell doors the night before. "Don't you sleep," was the mantra.

That kind of stuff went on for several days. I lost track of time, didn't know if it was day or night. Then suddenly, our "captors" charged into the cells, put hoods over our heads and marched us outside.

When they told us to pull off the hoods and started playing the Star Spangled Banner while raising the U.S. flag there wasn't a dry eye to be found. It was one of the moments where your heart is racing. You can hear it pounding in your ears. You feel alive, almost as if for the first time.

It was a moment I'll never forget.

Is it true you met your wife while going to flying school?

I met my wife on the way to survival school actually. Our meeting each other was fate. Destiny, if you believe in that type of thing.

When I returned from Japan, I had the opportunity to stop over in Seattle, Washington before going to Fairchild AFB. I hadn't been home to the United States in nearly three years, so I wanted to have a bit of fun before going to survival school. That's when I met my wife.

We got married six months later and have been married ever since.

What was Germany like?

Germany is a beautiful country, so much to see and do. The people are wonderful. I love German food. I miss the German meats, cheeses, and breads. I miss going to Saturday market, traveling to castles on the weekends. Everything.

For most of our stay, my wife and I lived in the upstairs flat of a small brick home in Kaiserslautern, Germany. We were within walking distance of a pub, bakery and delicatessen. On the weekend, an ice cream man would come through the neighborhood. He served Italian ice cream. Tiny little scoops. Dozens of flavors. For 5 Deutsche Mark, about $3 US, at the time, you could get a large waffle cone filled with those deliciously small scoops.

The early 1990's were a wild time to be in Germany. We were there when the Kaiserslautern soccer team became champions in Germany. The day they won was wild. Everyone ran through the streets shouting and cheering.

We were there for the whole build-up before and during the Gulf War. With all the terrorist threats and whatnot, it was a scary time to be overseas. Travel was restricted. Every time you went on base, they checked the car from end to end for explosives.

My wife was alone in Germany most of that time, as I was sent to the Gulf War. After the war, things slowly came back to normal, but it was a hard time.

The Soviet Union dissolved. The Berlin wall fell. The divided Germanies became one country. We saw it all first hand, my wife and I. It was an exciting time, but a dangerous time. So much potential unrest yet everywhere everyone was so excited. It was a great time to be alive, to know democracy and freedom.

Tell me more about the food in Europe.

You haven't tasted real food and drink till you've been to Europe, and Germany in particular. The Germans really know how to celebrate, and food and drink is at the center of it all.

It seems every village in Germany brews its own beer, makes its own wine. There's always a festival celebrating something and Oktoberfest is the biggest celebration of them all.

For us, it was expensive eating out but we loved the food so much we couldn't resist. Schnitzel and brown gravy has been one of my favorite meals ever since.

Our landlord was one of the nicest guys. Brilliant too. He spoke seven languages. He'd invite my wife and me over about once a week or so.

Did you travel in Europe?

My wife and I traveled as much as we could. The first year was bliss. We couldn't afford much. The base had discounted bus tours. We could also drive places to see things. One of our most memorable drives took us along the Rhine River. We visited castles as we went.

The first castle I ever visited was Frankenstein Castle. I couldn't resist visiting that one.

One of the benefits (or drawbacks depending on viewpoint) of being on airborne duty is that I had to go on a lot of temporary duty assignments. Those assignments took me all over Germany. I also went to England, Belgium, and Scotland.

I spent two perfect weeks at Mildenhall Airbase, England. Whenever I had a chance, I'd get in a rented car and head to London or Cambridge with some of the other aircrew members. Had you been there at the time you would have found me skulking about in the university libraries and pubs. The libraries had such wonderful books, and the pubs were the best place to meet students attending university.

My only regret was that my wife couldn't join me. As a member of the aircrew, I flew to

Mildenhall Airbase on our mission aircraft—the same plane we'd use in exercises on the temporary duty.

The one thing about England that I'll never forget is how friendly everyone is. I remember getting positively lost driving back from Cambridge one time. The person I was with suggested a just stop, roll down the window, and ask a passerby where to go. I laughed, said I knew where he tell me to go.

Boy was I wrong. The gentleman came straight over to the car and spent the next 5 minutes helping us find our way. He even let us use his pen so we could write down the directions.

How come you had to go to war?

When Iraq invaded Kuwait and the U.S. starting sending troops to the Middle East, I knew it might mean war. My father had been a freedom fighter in his native Hungary. My grandfather fought in the Spanish American War. I had relatives who served in World War I, World War II, the Korean War, and the Vietnam War.

I knew all about the Vietnam War and what a war in the Persian Gulf could mean, but I was never hesitant to do my duty. I volunteered to be among the first troops from our unit sent to the Gulf War and I was—even though the thought of war terrified me, and still does. Duty, honor, and country is the soldier's motto.

For me, it was a decision I had to make. It seemed the right choice then and it still does now. There are times in life when you have to make a choice. You can do nothing, or you can do something. I decided I wanted to do something.

Was it scary?

It wasn't only scary. It was terrifying. Words cannot describe or do justice to the horror of war. On my first mission, an Iraqi jet fighter launched against the plane I was flying in. I knew the capabilities of that fighter. I knew about the air-to-air missiles it carried. The gun canon used for strafing and close fighting.

That day I promised God that if he let me live I'd change my life. Do the things I said I would but never did. Become the person I should have become long ago.

That day was the first of many such. We had surface-to-air missiles launched against us several times. We had to fly through zones alive with anti-aircraft artillery fire.

Anyone who says they weren't terrified in such moments wouldn't be telling the truth. I was terrified. I still remember those dreadful times when I close my eyes sometimes.

But I wouldn't give those experiences back. I don't want to forget that time. Not even a moment of it. The Gulf War is a part of who I am. I earned the Distinguished Flying Cross, the United States of America's top flying honor, for my service.

Tell me about Hawaii.

My next assignment after the Gulf war was to Kunia Field Station, Hawaii. Kunia is an underground facility, carved under a hillside. During World War II, they made fighter aircraft in that facility. The fighter planes were flown out of Wheeler Army Air Station.

The Hawaiian Islands really are the pearls of the Pacific. It was a fortuitous assignment, more so than I knew at the time. My health deteriorated after the Gulf War. It was a secret I shared with few people. It wasn't manly to be sick that much. I didn't know what was happening to me. I only knew that I was taking sick frequently, but then in days or weeks I'd get better and everything would be fine for a while. I'd get strange rashes sometimes too. I remember getting a rash all around my eyes one time, that was the first symptom of the sickness for me.

My wife and I decided to have our first child around this time, and she suffered through three miscarriages. When she was carrying my son, she nearly lost him in the early weeks of pregnancy. I had to rush her to the hospital twice.

Years later I discovered that the thing I was experiencing had a name: Gulf War Syndrome. No one really understands it though. Some think it's a side effect of things soldiers were exposed to in the Gulf. Some think it's a side effect of the experimental drugs we took as a precaution against chemical and biological warfare agents. Some think it is the result of prolonged stress. Others think there's no such thing.

I personally think there is such a thing but I don't think we'll ever know for certain what causes it. I do believe, though, that if it weren't for Hawaii I wouldn't have made it through the years that followed the Gulf War. Some of my friends didn't make it.

But it wasn't a sad time on the whole. The weather in Hawaii is beautiful all year round. The sun and gentle climate are soothing. There is beauty everywhere. I was lucky to get stationed there. Someone really was watching over me and I do believe God answered my prayers.

During the same years that my health was privately falling apart, I got my "public" life together. The public and private me were two different people. I was afraid to share my secret pain. My career in the military was soaring. I earned several promotions, became our unit's technician of the year, and was on the road to Officer's Training School.

Academically, I was soaring too. Twice the military sent me to school, paying for my education. I went to six months of language classes at the University of Hawaii. I applied for and was accepted into the bootstrap program. I was one of two airmen selected for career and academic excellence, and given the opportunity to go to college full-time for a year.

The Dean of Hawaii Pacific University, the private college I attended, also granted me special permission to enter a dual-track degree program, allowing me to work on my master's degree at the same time I was completing my bachelor's degree.

The next year, I was the runner-up for class valedictorian and earned my bachelor's degree with top honors. The following year, I completed the master's program, earning my master's degree with distinction.

What made you want to get a degree, finally?

I made a decision during the Gulf War to turn my life around. Getting a degree was one of those things that I had said I would do but never had. I had tried before, but my heart was never in it. The problem is you need a degree to get ahead in life, and not only in whatever career you choose.

The extra years of education really do help mature a person. The rigor of study teaches more than is apparent. You also become more worldly wise, and hopefully more open-minded about the things you will see, do, and experience in life. You also have to learn discipline—you know: self-restraint, control, the ability to make the tough decisions. Things like not going out or watching television when you should study.

When I attended college classes in Japan, I was head of the class in Couch Potato 101. Let me tell you, it gets you nowhere. If I had completed my bachelor's degree in Japan when I started taking college classes, I would have been on the road to Officer's Training School 10 years earlier than actually happened.

But I was too thick skulled to understand. I thought that my job in the military was everything, that if I worked hard, I should be able to play hard. What I didn't understand was that as satisfying and challenging as the job was—and it was certainly both satisfying and challenging to direct intelligence operations—it was only a starting point in life and not an end point.

To get somewhere in life, I needed to drive there, myself. The gas for the car on that drive was a degree. It got me on the road to a better life.

Why did you leave the military?

The military is the best place for someone who has a dream or wants to find one. I can't imagine not having served, and it was truly a privilege.

Both of my degrees are in Computer Science. At the time, I was running the computer operations and analysis for our section, temporarily filling the position of a GS-15 who had returned to the states.

We were upgrading our entire operations, building a state of the art fiber optic network, backed by massive server arrays and high-power workstations. I was also training the new administration and analysis staff on everything from server installation to trouble shooting. It was a huge opportunity to put to use what I had learned in my degree programs.

One day near the end of the upgrade I came into the office and the GS-15's replacement was there. I had known that day would come. It was my job to help him transition. It was also the time when I had a decision to make: to stay in the military or to move on.

If I stayed in the military, I knew I wanted to become an officer. I had already completed my Officer's Training School package. I had full approval and was preparing for the training. Still it wasn't an easy decision, and one I didn't make until I had the completed package in my hand and was preparing to deliver it. In fact, I made the decision during the drive to drop off the package. I realized that as great as the military was and as exciting as it was to do what I did, it wasn't the best place for me.

When I made that decision, it was one of the hardest decisions I've ever had to make. Thinking about moving on, uprooting yourself and your family is terrifying. No one wants to start over in the middle of their life. It's like realizing that you've been standing in the wrong line for the past 30 years and now you've got to take a number and go to the end of a new line.

But that's exactly what I was doing when I decided to leave the military. I was starting over, moving back to square one, but I believed it was the right decision—and I still do.

There are times in life when you have to make a decision to move on or to keep doing what you are doing. The hardest, toughest, yet truest decision might be to move on, but you have to be willing to remake yourself, to put in the same long hours you did when you were just starting out, and you have to believe that you can achieve what you set out to achieve.

Writing Career

When did you first start writing about Ruin Mist?

For years, I had been thinking of the characters of Vilmos, Adrina, and Seth. I had this notion of three characters with very different backgrounds that would band together to stop a coming darkness.

Shortly after being stationed in Japan in 1986, I was sitting alone in my barracks room. I had just worked the midnight shift and I couldn't sleep. I turned on the computer, an Amiga 500 that I had bought my senior year of high school.

I started out with the intention of writing a letter home, but when I turned on the computer I got sidetracked. After a time, I was just sitting there staring at the blank screen. The word processor was started. The blank page and the blinking cursor seemed an invitation. For some reason, I don't know why, an image of Princess Adrina came into my mind's eye. She was standing atop a wall, staring out into the world. I started typing, and the words just came:

> Summer must surely be at an end, Adrina surmised, for the breeze came from the North and not from the direction of the West Deep.

I stopped there. Suddenly, all the ideas I had been thinking about for years were coming together in my mind. I turned away from the keyboard, grabbed a notebook and pen. I wrote down all my thoughts, started putting the disconnected pieces together. Within several weeks, I filled the notebook and started another. The ideas kept flowing.

I knew almost immediately that the story I had to tell couldn't be told in a single book. I was writing the background history and story ideas for a series of books, and one idea in particular stuck in my mind: the notion of a world where the history was subject to interpretation. There are two sides to every story, and I knew that the world I was inventing had to have two sets of histories.

I spent the next three years writing the history and the stories. I finished writing the first book and hundreds of pages of history before I showed anyone what I'd written.

When did you first try to get the Ruin Mist books published?

I'd been tinkering with writing for many years. I'd written stories, but never anything longer than a few pages. I'd never tried to get any of my stories published and the idea of getting published never crossed my mind when I started writing about Adrina and her friends.

Years passed. I kept writing, and by the early 1990's I had several completed manuscripts and many hundreds of pages of history for the world I called Ruin Mist. It wasn't until the Persian Gulf War that I found focus in my life, however. My wife played a large part in that, but the war also.

The war gave me time to retrospect on what I'd accomplished in my life, and up until that time, it wasn't much. I had wasted my talents. I hadn't done anything I said I was going to do with my life.

I subscribed to Writer's Digest for the first time and began reading books on how to get published. In 1991, after reading about an essay contest, I submitted a story and won.

Winning the contest gave me the courage to write a proposal that I sent to publishers, but I think most of the publishers who received the proposal dismissed it offhand. I was an unknown, unpublished writer who was trying to sell a series of books. I didn't have an agent, either.

The inevitable rejections didn't dissuade me from continuing; they only strengthened my resolve. I studied the industry more, tried to correspond with writers I respected, like it says in some of the books on getting published.

Let me tell you though, firsthand, that chivalry is dead. None of the writers I wrote for advice ever wrote back.

In 1993, I sent out very selective query letters to individual publishers. I got strong interest from Tor. An editor asked for the complete manuscript and we started corresponding. But Tor ultimately decided to not to publish, and I kept trudging on.

The next submission got a direct response from the executive editor. The editor stated, "The fantasy world you have created is truly wonderful and rich. Your characters seem real and full of life." The story I created wasn't right for the publisher's line of books, however. I quickly discovered that other publishers weren't sure how to fit the book in their list either.

In fantasy books, epic quests like Terry Brook's Shannara were what publishers were publishing and readers were buying. Publishers had no idea what to do with the type of story I had written.

The books at their heart were a story of intrigue between two powerful families: the House of Alder and the House of Tyr'anth. Epic quests were a part of the story, but they weren't *the* story.

In some versions of the work, I submitted the story of Adrina, Vilmos, and Seth as separate chapters. Chapter 1 began Adrina's story. Chapter 2, Vilmos'. Chapter 3, Seth's. Chapter 4 continued Adrina's story, Chapter 5 Vilmos' and so on. I was told that approach would never sell. No one would ever buy a book where the story switched to a different character every chapter. But if you read current fiction you know how wrong they were about that.

Based on the strong disapproval of the idea, I revised the manuscripts and tried different approaches. Eventually though, I ended up right where I started, which was frustrating.

By 1995, I was just about to give up the dream of getting published when I got my first big break: I sold an editor on a proposal for a technical how-to book—something I knew very well. That led to my career as a technical how-to writer.

What happened after your first book was published?

The publisher I was working with really liked that book. Before it was published, I was already contracted to write a second book. By the time the first book was in stores, I was writing the second book. At the time, 1995, I was in the military, completing my degree, and trying to meet the deadlines for the second book—any one of which was a full-time job by itself.

I had a 3-year old running around the house and we didn't have a room where I could work in private. I set up my desk in the living room, a few feet from the TV. I adapted, blocked out the distractions and got the work done. Looking back, the best part of it all was that I was surrounded by family at that stressful time.

In 1996, I decided not to pursue a career as a military officer and got out of the Air Force. At the same time, my publisher was adapting my bestselling how-to book and I was writing additional materials for a professional reference edition.

The publisher also packaged that edition with software titles, creating the Professional Web Design Kit and the Web Publishing Electronic Resource Kit.

Tell me about the publication of the first Ruin Mist book.

In 2000, I created a 5-year strategy for publishing the Ruin Mist books. The goal was to publish the first books in Winter 2001.

I had everything lined up so the first two books, *Keeper Martin's Tale* and *The Kingdoms & the Elves of the Reaches*, would be published in Winter 2001, followed by the next two books, *Elf Queen's Quest* and *The Kingdoms & The Elves of the Reaches II*, in Spring 2002. The catastrophe on September 11, 2001 changed those plans.

We pushed back publication of the first two books, and changed the launch strategy completely. We even went with a different publishing strategy. Missing the entire Christmas shopping season was disheartening.

It felt like the past two years of work toward publication were wasted, but that feeling changed quickly. The Spring 2002 launch was a success. *Keeper Martin's Tale* and *Elf Queen's Quest* climbed online bestseller lists almost immediately and stayed there for over 6 weeks.

Inquiries for translation, motion picture, and audio rights started to pour in. I had many offers but ultimately accepted none of the initial offers. I was too busy with the other Ruin Mist books, and it was too early to sell some of the rights. The timing just didn't feel right.

I let the deals pass. I don't know if it was the right choice, but it felt like it at the time.

How many Ruin Mist books will there be?

I've already written the first drafts of *Fields of Honor*, *Mark of the Dragon*, and two additional adult Ruin Mist books. But I believe that *Mark of the Dragon* and its young adult counterparts, *In the Service of Dragons* I and II, will probably be the last of the books I publish.

In my mind, that is where the story should end. Readers may change my mind about that, but for now, that is what I believe.

Of the hundreds of pages of history, the most interesting to me is the history of the

Second Siege. That story alone could fill several books, so perhaps that could be another series. For now, I don't really know. Readers will have to let me know what they think.

What will you do when you publish the last Ruin Mist book?

I'll probably take a vacation. I don't go on many, and I'll surely need a break by that time. I think I'll be sad. Finishing that last book will be like parting with old friends—family. I'll miss it.

Afterward, I know I'll have to move on to other books. Writing pays the bills. I don't think I'll ever achieve the success of J.R.R. Tolkien, or J.K. Rowling, so I will literally have to keep working. It won't be a choice.

If I'm lucky though, I'll be able to afford a long vacation. I'd love to be able to spend a month on a secluded island with my family, nothing to do, and no worries. Hey, it's a dream. Everyone has to have a dream. Right?

The Ruin Mist Books

An overview

Who are the main characters?

The Ruin Mist books are foremost a story of a struggle for power. In the kingdoms, King Andrew and King Jarom fight for control, and there is intrigue, plotting, and scheming.

King Andrew is the patriarch of House Alder. The main characters in this family are King Andrew's children:

Adrina..........Youngest daughter of King Andrew. She is becoming a woman and has many concerns for her future and that of her family.

Midori..........Daughter of King Andrew who has been exiled. Her given name is Delinna. She took the name Midori after becoming a priestess.

Valam..........Only son of King Andrew, also known as the Lord and Prince of the South.

Calyin..........Oldest daughter of King Andrew. She lives in the far north with her husband the Lord of the North.

King Jarom is the patriarch of House Tyr'anth. In the early books not much information is provided about this powerful family. That changes as Emel makes his way through the southern kingdoms, and as King Jarom's plots become bolder.

Other characters in the books hail from places within and beyond the kingdoms. These characters include:

Emel..........Young guardsman who is one of Adrina's closest friends.

Galan..........Elf from East Reach across the great sea.

Jacob..........A priest of the father and friend to House Alder.

Martin..........A keeper of the lore, and guardian of the ancient texts and knowledge.

Seth..........Elf from East Reach across the great sea.

Vilmos..........Young boy from Tabborrath Village in Sever. Sever is one of the southern kingdoms.

William..........Prince of Sever who becomes king after his father's death.

Xith..........Vilmos' benefactor who rescues him and leads him away from his homeland.

These characters have significant parts to play in the books, but they are not the only characters in the books. Other characters you'll see include Edward Tallyback, the troant, Myrial, the servant girl, and Ansh Brodst, captain of the Imtal guard.

How does the author manage so many characters?

It is a challenge to create so many diverse characters and maintain their identities, but the many characters help breathe life into the story. The characters' lives are interesting, and they each have their own concerns, likes, and dislikes. They give the plot depth and make the world feel real.

Whenever readers write to Robert Stanek, they tell him about their favorite characters. Sometimes they tell him how worried they are for a particular character. He especially likes hearing about characters that readers can really identify with.

The character everyone seems to identify most strongly with is Adrina. Most readers understand her great sadness over the loss of her mother and how it has affected her life. In the third book, there is a dark scene where Adrina faces her demons, and Robert Stanek has heard from more than a few readers about that scene.

Seth, Emel, and Vilmos also have a lot of fans. Of these three, the one character that the author was initially unsure of was Emel. Emel is Adrina's dearest friend. They've been getting in trouble together since they were toddlers. In the original planning for the first book, he had a small part, but as the author got into the writing, there was so much chemistry between Adrina and Emel that he expanded the role. Emel is a favorite of many readers.

It gladdens the author's heart when readers also understand and sympathize with minor characters. A lot of readers love Edward Tallyback and they want nothing more than for him to come back and play King's Mate with Vilmos. Unfortunately, that would be difficult given Edward's current condition, so the only thing we can tell these fans is that Vilmos will play

King's Mate again and the game will have a much more significant role in the story when he does.

Myrial is another minor character that readers are particularly fond of. Her character originally had a very small part to play in the books, but, like Emel, she came to life on the page, so much so that the author expanded her role.

So as you can see, Robert Stanek manages the characters as though they were real people. Every character in every book has a history, a past. Sometimes what he writes onto the page, the things they do in the story, changes what he originally saw as their future. Because of this, their roles in the story change.

How come the Ruin Mist world has differing histories?

Like the author has said before, there are two sides to every story. Our version of a story may be different from yours, even if we're witnessing the same events. Now, if we're talking about history, the stories from opposing societies and peoples are often very different. The contrast may be as different as night and day.

In our own history, we're starting to see how very different viewpoints can be.

What is the dark place Vilmos visits?

Ruin Mist has three distinct realms of existence: Under-Earth, Middle-Earth and Over-Earth. Under-Earth, with its blood-red skies and lack of sun, moon, or stars, is a dark place at first blush. But as you get a deeper, better understanding of this otherworldly realm, you may see it in a different light. Literally.

Where do the dragons and titans live?

Over-Earth is the home of dragons and titans. But don't forget about the eagle lords. Those three are the great races of Ruin Mist's past.

At the dawn of the first age, it was the titan Ky'el who gave the lesser races (men, elves, and dwarves) their freedom—at a great cost to himself and his people. Before that, the lesser races were slaves to the greater races (dragons, titans and eagle lords).

Over the millennia, knowledge of Over-Earth's existence faded from the memory of the living, even that of the long-lived elves and dwarves. Most believe it is a place of myth and legend, and that it never truly existed. That's all we can say without giving away too much of the story in later books.

How come men and elves are enemies in Ruin Mist?

Men and elves have a rich history together as friends and foes. In the time of Ky'el, men and elves labored side by side catering to the whims of their masters. But by the dawn of the Second Age, men and elves became the masters of their own lands and kingdoms. Thanks to Ky'el and his great sacrifice.

A peaceful time followed, but that peace was broken by Dnyarr, Elf King of Greye. Dnyarr united the elves against men, and that betrayal was the greatest in the long history of Ruin Mist. That betrayal is the reason men and elves are divided. There is more of course, but the true secrets are revealed in the books over the course of the story.

What is the significance of the Ruin Mist book covers?

The book covers are symbolic, especially the early covers. Since the publisher didn't have a lot of funds to create the covers, the author designed the covers himself. He still does, but now he does it more because he enjoys it.

With the *Keeper Martin's Tales* series, the symbolism revolves around water. While we won't reveal what it means, we will point out the symbols and the scenes:

Book 1 Shows a waterfall in contrasting light. A great shadow is over the waterfall, yet at the edges there is bright sunlight. In the original hardcover edition and the recent trade editions, the author was able to expand this and fulfill his original vision. Those covers show twin waterfalls in contrasting light. If you look closely between the falls, you'll see three shapes emerging from the shadows.

Book 2 Provides a view into a hidden glen where a great waterfall pours into a hidden lake. The view is through trees. Sunlight on the trees makes them bright while the background has a bit of shadow over it.

Book 3 Depicts a fast-running stream. The streambed is full of rocks and the water is churning, running white through the scene. The surrounding area is rich and green, and there are delicate yellow flowers in the midst of the raging water.

Teacher's Classroom Guide: The Ruin Mist Books

Book 4   Shows a raging waterfall and a wall of water racing out from the rocky mountainside. Three shapes are depicted in front of the wall of water and behind them is a great gray swirl. If you look closely, you see two separate rivers merging into one, which is split into two falls by a great stone dragon's head. At the top of the stone is a circle of stone and within the circle are six warriors clad in blue. Part of the image is reversed and obscured.

With the Ruin Mist Tales, the symbolism is different. Again we won't reveal what it means, but we will point out the symbols and the scenes:

Book 1   Shows a lake with forest-covered mountains and a clear sky with a few patches of clouds. In the original hardcover edition and the recent trade editions, the author was able to expand this and fulfill his original vision. Those covers show a river and an access way between two stone walls. If you look closely between the pillars of stone, you'll see several shadowy shapes in the green folds of the forest. In the heavens above, there are identical cloud formations and two eagles far off in the distance.

Book 2   Depicts a cloud-shrouded mountain. At the base of the mountain is a forest covered in a dark shadow. As before, the original hardcover edition and the recent trade editions expanded on this theme and vision. Those covers show a plateau of yellow and red stones. If you look closely, three shapes are depicted in the red stones, and the forest atop plateau depicts a single shape with its upper limbs outstretched. The pattern in the clouds above may catch your eye as well.

With the Ruin Mist Chronicles, the symbols are very detailed in the art on the original trade paperbacks, less so in the hardcovers, but all the symbols are significant. Let's look at the art covers first:

Book 1   Provides an imaginary view off the shores of the West Deep, not far from Alderan. The rock formation shown is called the Maiden. She stands between two great walls of rocks and the waves crash inward at the shore all around her. The sun is setting. The tide, turning. And there are dark clouds in the sky. If you look closely, several figures will be revealed. The first and foremost is a hooded figure with his hands held out in front of him, gripping a fine sword pointed down. Behind this figure is a watery king with a crown of waves and a beard of shimmering water pools. The maiden, with her arms down and outstretched, is of course a figure in the picture as well. At the base of the Maiden figure are two ghastly countenances.

Book 3   Provides an imaginary view into the Dead Sea near the Cliffs of D'Ardynne. The rock formation shown is called Heartbreak, which is in the middle of Desolation Bay. An immense, dark waterspout is racing into the bay, causing the water to churn, and bringing waves crashing into the shore. The sun is setting. The tide, turning. Heartbreak itself is said to depict three figures: the winged lord come to save Alexia as she fell from the cliffs, the doomed Alexia herself, and the creature risen from the depths to drag her to a watery grave.

With the Ruin Mist Chronicle hardcovers and successive books, the images seem much simpler but are just as significant. Here's what you should look for and a few insights:

Book 1   Shows crossed tridents. The clouds flowing around the clenched fists and the tridents themselves depict several figures. Note that a trident has three forks. When you show two tridents together as in the picture, there are six forks. The numbers 2, 3, and 6 are significant, and are part of the theme in many of the covers. If you look closely, you'll see several figures in the clouds. In the center of the picture is a figure with outstretched arms and a large hat. Above this figure, as if newly risen, is the figure of a great winged bird or beast. Look also at the spine to see how the symbols are revealed when the figure is inverted.

Book 2   Provides a view to a secret lake and island through trees. The trees on the island are in neat rows. If you look closely though, you will see a shadowy figure in the outline of the trees. Beyond the secret island are two banks of clouds, which are mirrors of each other that merge at a central gray mass: a dark storm in the distance. You'll also see shadows on the forest-covered mountains surrounding the lake.

Book 3   Shows the Guardians of the Kingdoms. These stone behemoths are hunched down with their hands on their knees. If you look closely, you'll see several shadowy figures. Between the two hands of each guardian is a priest in a hooded robe, kneeling, with hands clasped in prayer. Above the priest is a figure, and above that, a winged beast. There are other figures to find as well.

The publisher and author hope to be able to continue creating these kinds of covers, but it is a lot of work. It'd be much easier to slap on a cover with a few warriors and a maiden or something. Ultimately, readers make the decision for the publisher. If they want to see more traditional covers, that's what the publisher will use.

What is King's Mate?

King's Mate is one of the oldest forms of entertainment in the kingdoms. The history of the game goes all the way back to the days of Antwar Alder, the first ruler of Great Kingdom.

In those days, lords and royals played the game. Each of the pieces was represented by an actual person who moved around a life-size white- and black-marble playing field.

As the years faded one into the other, the game was forgotten until King Antwar Alder IX rediscovered the game. His scholars and master class soldiers quickly followed, and they played the game heavily in the early years after the revival.

Within a generation, common soldiers were playing the game as well, and then the passion for the game spread throughout the kingdoms. It is said that there is no corner of the kingdoms where the game is not now played.

Ruin Mist
in Schools

Ruin Mist in Schools

Good books become a part of our lives. The best seem like old friends. They contain words and characters that inspire us. They give us insights and provide new views of our world, and they can do this even if they are themselves windows into entirely new worlds. In the Ruin Mist books, Robert Stanek provides such a window, and readers around the world are discovering and cherishing the books.

Teachers have discovered the books as well. They've learned that the books have stories to tell beyond the typed page. The books are windows into the heart, mind, and soul. They tell stories of friendship, loyalty, and compassion.

Through the character of Seth, the books explore prejudice and its devastating effects. Through the character of Adrina, the books explore grief and healing. The message in every book is clear, and ultimately life-affirming: good can triumph over evil, hard work has rewards, and everyone has the opportunity to make a difference.

Exploring Ruin Mist in the Classroom

With so many Ruin Mist books, choosing which book to use in the classroom may be a difficult. You can start with *The Kingdoms and the Elves of the Reaches*, and invite your students to continue reading books 2, 3, and 4 on their own.

Both girls and boys enjoy the stories. Girls seem to like Princess Adrina the most, and they are very interested in her friendship with Emel. Boys seem to like the characters of Vilmos and Seth the most, especially when they discover Vilmos is a boy their age and Seth is an elf.

Before you begin, you may want to discuss the difference between a fantasy and a realistic novel. The world of Ruin Mist is an imaginary place. Magic is an important part of the story in the Ruin Mist books, as it is with most fantasy, including classic fairy tales like Cinderella, Snow White, and even Pinocchio. Magic is what brings Pinocchio to life, and it's what makes Pinocchio's nose grow when he lies.

Then, do some pre-reading activities with the class. Activities that might work well in your class include:

- Ask the students what they think when they hear the words "The Kingdoms and the Elves of the Reaches." Note their responses and then tell them that is the title of the book they are about to read.
- Find out if your students have heard of Robert Stanek, and if they know anything about his personal life or his writing. You may want to read some of the questions and answers from the section of this text entitled "An Interview with Robert Stanek."
- Shows students the maps of The Reaches and Great Kingdom at the beginning of the book. Ask students what they think about some of the place names on the maps, such as the West Deep, the Dead Sea, and the Isle of Silence.
- Have students answer these questions:
  1. Are you interested in:
     - stories of fantasy and magic?
     - struggles between good and evil?
     - ways people can change the world?
     - sacrifices heroes make to save others?
  2. Have you ever:
     - wished things were different in your life?
     - had a scary dream that made you wake up?
     - gone on a long trip but were unsure about it?
     - regretted fighting with a friend?

Expanding Vocabulary

Like other works of fiction, Robert Stanek's *The Kingdoms and the Elves of the Reaches* will help expand students' vocabulary. You can help your students learn and retain these words by providing interesting activities.

Activities that you may want to try include:

- Challenge your students to look up new words in the dictionary and write down the meanings after reading each chapter. Have your students alphabetize the words and create a glossary.
- Use new words as part of a weekly vocabulary test, or challenge your students to a

weekly vocabulary bee that uses the words in a particular chapter. Ask your students to define the words as well as spell them.

- Give your students the opportunity to practice their writing skills by using the words in sentences and paragraphs. Afterward, have students share their work with the class.
- Play 20 Questions or Vocabulary Charades. With 20 Questions, one student selects a vocabulary word and gives clues about it while other students ask questions and try to guess the word. With Vocabulary Charades, one student selects a vocabulary word and acts it out while other students try to guess the word.

Next, you'll find lists of vocabulary words, organized by chapter.

Chapter 1

Feral	Trustworthy	Dominate
Edifice	Surreptitiously	Levitate
Portcullis	Feat	Solitude
Fleeting	Warden	Indignity
Ransom	Century	
Incursion	Ancestral	

Chapter 2

Conscious	Governess	Somber
Chamber	Justification	Cognizant
Principal (Adj.)	Obvious	Imaginary
Habitual	Sympathize	Unfulfilled
Dreary	Contemplate	Conjure
Tradition	Courtier	Sanctuary
Abandon	Aloof	Announcement
Independent	Persistent	Insatiable
Maternal	Meditation	Acknowledgement

Chapter 3

Occurrence	Retribution	Merciless
Oscillate	Perplex	Befuddlement
Eavesdrop	Permeate	Injustice
Breach	Defiance	Aimlessly
Ethics	Malice	Adolescence
Accompany	Preordained	Insignia
Prescient	Encounter	Spontaneous
Unwholesome	Temptation	
Intuitive	Perish	

Chapter 4

Plague	Discount
Endearing	Perfunctory
Baritone	Melodramatic
Mysterious	Competition
Reverent	Standards
Defensive	Pristine
Etiquette	Judgment

Chapter 5

Complacent	Lingering	Bewildered
Perpetually	Mocking	Charismatic
Relinquish	Pensive	Remorse
Sermon	Methodical	Enchantment
Intervene	Perfunctory	Rebuke
Impart	Consciously	Crescendo
Wisdom	Lingering	Dissipate
Commitment	Sinister	Sepulchral

Chapter 6

Errant	Recruit	Clamber
Inevitable	Sergeant	Appearance
Pittance	Congratulate	Serenity
Gallant	Betrothal	Ponderous
Invasion	Wayward	Spectacle
Consequence	Diminish	Spectacular
Unbearable	Cobbled	

Chapter 7

Torture	Companion	Somber
Overshadow	Destination	Ration
Vigor	Beguile	Utmost
Nervously	Elude	Gibbous
Stammer	Shaman	Stark
Sympathetic	Saddlebag	Hostile

Chapter 8

Guidance	Monotonous	Raucous
Occasional	Subordinate	Reprieve
Dismount	Distinguish	Flatter
Communicate	Dishearten	Embarrassment
Predecessor	Lackluster	Proposition
Aftertaste	Apprenticeship	Influence
Petty	Flagging	Traitor

Chapter 9

Escort	Foremast	Ironic
Blockade	Lateen	Instantaneous
Engulf	Galleon	Ferocity
Boatswain	Broadside	Laceration
Engagement	Rend	Founder
Dedicated	Grapple	Yearn

Chapter 10

Suspicious	Incantation	Forbidden
Descent	Cacophony	Succumb
Punishment	Procession	Destructive
Distinctive	Unmistakable	Knotted
Betray	Appeal	Melancholy
Quotation	Enthusiastic	Whittle
Teleport	Education	

Chapter 11

Traversable	Preoccupy	Aggravate
Infrequent	Recuperate	Tributary
Independent	Awareness	Detachment
Peddler	Extensive	Sheepishly
Holding (N.)	Company	Dilapidated
Fortunate	Column	Complement
Commander	Whinny	

Chapter 12

Sprawling	Boundless
Brambles	Glistening
Gradually	Objective
Progress	Staggered
Interval	Saturated
Overwhelming	Infection
Rationalize	Terrifying

Chapter 13

Customary	Coordinated
Mire	Sentinel
Deficient	Suppressed
Putrid	Misleading
Vegetation	Tumultuous
Insurance	Wanton
Portentous	Excruciating

Chapter 14

Cautiously	Reverently	Behemoth
Content	Twinge	Hearth
Arcane	Aspiration	Assortment
Clapboarded	Profound	Generation
Exterior	Periodically	Jaded
Elongated	Impressionable	Grimace
Respective	Coastal	Perish

Chapter 15

Disaster	Overcast	Devastating
Despair	Frazzled	Treachery
Turbulent	Haggard	Infection
Desperate	Debris	Concentrated
Fatigue	Invaluable	Huddled
Exhaustion	Waned	
Anguish	Horizon	

Chapter 16

Haphazardly	Litany
Attention	Rhythmic
Uniform	Noticeable
Miracle	Convulse
Reassuring	Comfortable
Instinctively	Unsettling

Teacher's Classroom Guide Robert Stanek's Ruin Mist

Learning Creatively

Class projects can help ensure that each student's reading of *The Kingdoms and the Elves of the Reaches* is a unique experience that touches them personally. Class projects can also help students better understand, summarize, and review the book.

A few ideas for class projects include:

- **Reading Journals**   Ask students to create a journal for *The Kingdoms and the Elves of the Reaches*. Don't grade the journal. Instead make it an activity that allows students to reflect without being corrected or worrying about a letter grade. Tell the students that the purpose of the journal is to record any thoughts, ideas, or questions they might have as they read *The Kingdoms and the Elves of the Reaches*. If any students need help getting started, ask them to write one or more things they learned after reading each chapter, or ask them to write about a character or event that was in the chapter they just read. To show students that you are reviewing the journal, enter nonjudgmental comments or use stickers, such as smiley faces where they've done a good job expressing themselves.

- **Individual Projects**   Ask students to choose a scene from the book and illustrate it, or to create a map of a certain place in Ruin Mist, such as Imtal Palace. Suggest that they reread the chapter containing the scene they want to use before they get started. If they want to illustrate several scenes, they could create a picture book to share with the class or others.

- **Partner Projects**   Select intriguing scenes or interesting paragraphs from *The Kingdoms and the Elves of the Reaches*. You should have one scene or paragraph for every two students in the class. Pair each student with a partner and have them read the scene or paragraph. Ask the students to read and discuss the scene or paragraph with their partner, and then write in their own words what they think it means. Encourage students to think of different ways the scene or paragraph could be interpreted and to illustrate their work as well.

Teacher's Classroom Guide Robert Stanek's Ruin Mist

Playing King's Mate in the Classroom

King's Mate is very similar to chess. Game play is challenging and can make for hours of enjoyment. If students are interested in playing the game, have them start by making the game pieces and board. A student with a rudimentary knowledge of chess can begin playing King's Mate almost immediately.

You'll need 24 game pieces:

2 Kings	The white king has an oversized, jeweled crown on its head and a sheathed sword in its right hand. The black king wears a dark cape with a singlet for a crown and holds a scepter in its left hand. Placed in the raised square in the center of the last row on each end.
4 Swordmasters	Swordmasters are knights with a sword raised high into the air. They occupy a square on either side of the king and may move any number of spaces, but must always be adjacent to the king. They revolve around the king and rotate around his moves, moving always in direct lines. One must always be in an adjacent square touching the king and the other may be adjacent to the king or the other swordmaster.
2 Priests	The priest wears a long, collared cape with white or black insignia and is placed next to the left Swordmaster.
2 Priestesses	The priestess wears a long, hooded cloak of black or white and is placed next to the right Swordmaster.
4 Keepers	Keepers carry a thick, bound book above their heads as if a shield. Keepers are placed on the last squares on the end to the left and right.
10 Fools	Five fools are placed in the row in front of the king. From the left, they are placed in the 1st, 2nd, 4th, 6th and 7th columns, leaving empty spaces in front of the swordmasters.

Students can create the pieces using cardboard cutouts and stands. Or, for convenience, you can use standard chess pieces with nametags taped on each to identify them. Here's how that would work:

- Discard the queens. These pieces aren't needed.
- Use the kings as kings.
- Use the knights as swordmasters.
- Use the bishops for the priest and priestess pieces.
- Use the rooks as keepers.
- Keep 5 pawns of each color for the fools.

The King's Mate game board has nine rows and seven columns from the player's perspective. You'll find seven raised areas on the board, five of which are in the center and form an 'X'. The remaining two are in the center of the last row on each end—these are the places for the dark and light kings.

Here's what the board looks like:

Movement of Pieces

Kings Kings move one space at a time, in any direction.

Swordmasters Swordmasters are like the queen pieces in chess. They may move any number of spaces in any direction—diagonally, vertically or horizontally. The catch is that one must always be in an adjacent square touching the king. The other may be adjacent to the king or the other swordmaster. Because of this, students will need to plan the moves for swordmasters and kings carefully.

Priest/Priestess Priests and priestesses are like bishops in chess. They move diagonally in one direction only, any number of spaces on a given turn. Unlike chess, the priest and the priestess are not placed on opposing colored squares.

Keepers Keepers are like rooks in chess. Keepers move vertically or horizontally, any number of spaces on a given turn.

Fools Fools are like pawns in chess, except that they may move forward or backward. Fools move one space at a time.

Capturing Pieces

You capture pieces according to the direction that the captor moves. Except for the fool—the fool only takes pieces that are diagonal to it. That is why he is called the fool, for he is the only piece that captures other pieces the opposite way that he moves.

The king cannot be captured until both his swordmasters are taken from him. So you must take both swordmasters in order to capture the king and win.

When a player's piece is in a position to take the other player's king, the king is said to be in check. However, unlike chess, the king can only be in check when both of his swordmasters have been taken by the other player.

As in chess, the game is over when one player's king is in check and can no longer move to get out of check. This is called checkmate.

Notes

The five raised squares in the center of the board have a special purpose:
- Only a king and his swordmasters may pass through the raised squares or stop on them. The only exception is when the player's king occupies one of these squares. At this time, any of the pieces of his color may cross or stop on the raised squares.
- As long as the king remains on that space, this remains true. If the king moves off the raised square, pieces of his color can no longer cross or stop on the raised squares. Note that any pieces already on a raised square can stay in their position. If the player moves a piece off the square, the normal rules resume.

The two raised squares in either end of the board are called the King Squares. They serve only to denote where the white and black kings start the game. In the expanded rules version of the game, however, there is a move called Fools Gambit.

Here how Fools Gambit works:
- If a player's fool occupies the King Square for his color, other fools of his color can cross or stop on any of the other raised squares on the board.
- The catch is that if the other player's fool gets on the opposing King Square he or she wins the game.

If you ask the question, "But how can you capture the king and win if you have to take the swordmasters first?" The answer you may receive from players is "Through patience, skill, and sacrifice." For nothing good can be gained otherwise, and that is the foundation of King's Mate.

Exploring Common Trades in the Kingdoms

In the kingdoms, men and women live and die by their tradecraft. Master craftsmen often become teachers and have many apprentices. An apprentice must train for several years before he can become a journeyman, and many journeymen do a lifetime's work without ever becoming masters of their craft.

Students may enjoy role playing or other activities that portray the lives of characters in the kingdoms. One way to do this is to discuss the common trades in the kingdoms and then let students chose a trade that they'd like to study. Students may enjoy researching these trades to see if they can find ties to trades in our own history.

Students may also enjoy making a fictional diary or journal of a person who lived during these times. They might imagine what it was like to be this person and have this role in society.

Bladefighters

Bladefighters are found throughout the kingdoms and the free cities. Another name for a bladefighter is a hired blade. As you might imagine, there are many places in the kingdoms where hired blades earn tidy sums for their work. If you need to hire many blades, best look to the free cities where they understand the true value of gold.

Blademaster	A master class bladesman. To become a blademaster, a bladesman must learn the trade of the weaponsmith, and after fashioning his own long blade, he must use that blade to defeat a magical beast, a champion or an outcast blademaster.
Bladesman	A skilled bladesman who earns a living by his long blade. Bladesmen are often called into the service of the crown.
Blade	An apprentice bladesman.

Booksmiths

In the early days of the kingdoms, many entered the booksmith trade, but as the ages pass, fewer and fewer young people enter the trade. With an ever dwindling population of booksmiths, master booksmiths have grown far and few between. If you need to find a master booksmith, you'd better travel to a major city.

Because of their access to books and libraries, closed to all save noblemen, master booksmiths typically are very learned and this learning and the passing of years gives them wisdom, which is highly sought after. Many master booksmiths are also advisors to the noble houses, where they are involved in the politics of the land.

Master Booksmith	A master class booksmith. To become a master booksmith, a booksmith must scribe and bind a book for a nobleman or lore keeper, who must in turn bestow the title of master booksmith.
Booksmith	A highly skilled scribe who is capable of writing and binding books. Some books, such as the Great Book of Sever, can take a lifetime to scribe.
Scribe	A writer of scrolls and often a producer of parchment. Scribes are highly regarded, for there are few commoners who can read and write.

Coachmen

Becoming a coachman is one of the only ways to safely see the greater world. Caravans are protected by armed escorts and kingdom soldiers. But the life of a coachman isn't all flowers and green fields. Coachmen are the last line of defense in protecting travelers from street bandits, thieves, and things that go bump in the night. Because of this, the best coachmen have also trained as bladesmen.

Carriagemaster	A master class coachman, typically in the service of nobility. To become a carriagemaster, a coachman must train as a bladesman, become skilled in close-range and long-range fighting, and then prove himself on a journey.
Coachman	A journeyman class, typically assisting a carriagemaster or acting as a carriage attendant.
Cart	An apprentice coachman.

Huntsmen

In cities, huntsmen rarely get the respect they deserve, but it is a foolish nobleman that keeps no huntsmen. For it is the huntsmen who learn the ins and outs of the wild country, the huntsmen who track the mysterious creatures that pass through the lands, and the huntsmen who learn how to trap what is needed when the winter snow chills the land.

A typical chief huntsman has a range, a given lot of land that he is responsible for keeping track of. The chief huntsman may assign senior huntsmen to look over parts of the land, but is ultimately responsible if something should happen within that range.

Chief Huntsman	A master class huntsman often in the employ of a noble family or great house. To become a chief huntsman, a huntsman must be appointed or must discredit the current huntsman and prove himself worthy of a promotion. Chief huntsmen are expert trackers and are skilled with many weapons, including bows and swords.
Huntsman	A journeyman class hunter who earns a living hunting wild game and tracking.
Hunter	An apprentice huntsman.

Linemen

Directing a caravan train is not a job for the faint of heart. Caravanmasters must understand strategy and field tactics if they are to outwit Mother Nature (storms, floods, and other natural phenomena) and the mix of thieves, cutthroats, and dark creatures that they'll encounter.

The best caravanmasters can create elaborate travel plans from two pieces of information: The starting point and the ending point of the journey. To be successful, the caravanmaster must be able to hire bladesmen, obtain supplies (food, horses, wagons, etc.) and complete the journey without causing or sustaining injury or losing the goods.

Caravanmaster	A master class lineman, typically in charge of a caravan train bringing supplies to Kingdom cities and outposts. To become a caravanmaster, a lineman must survive the trade, follow the prescribed rules, and earn the trust of the garrison commander responsible for the routes traveled. If a garrison commander is willing to put his mark on a lineman's caravan plans, the lineman has earned the promotion to master.
Lineman	A journeyman class, typically responsible for a section of a caravan train.
Liner	An apprentice lineman.

Ridesmen

Ridesmen are found throughout the kingdoms and the free cities. It is a highly valued trade, as horses and other beasts of burden are the primary means of transporting people and goods. In the Kingdoms of Yug and Zapad, many exotic animals are used for riding, including elephants, zebras, and king cats. King cat riders can also be found in Vostok.

Ridemaster	A master class ridesman. To become a ridemaster, a ridesman must be able to tame any and all beasts of burden, from the wildest stallion to the exotic mounts of the southern kingdoms. But taming beasts of burden is only the beginning; ridemasters are showmen, earning the respect of the crowd with their skills, and teachers, able to teach proper riding technique to commoners, and lords and ladies alike.
Ridesman	A skilled rider who earns his living doing show riding or horse taming.
Rider	An apprentice ridesman.

Shipwrights

Most shipwrights earn their pay and respect in coastal towns, building merchant fleets and military craft. Some live and work along the great rivers of the kingdoms. Master Shipwright Armon, who discovered the Mouth of the World, is said to have been the greatest shipwright that ever lived. Hundreds of years later, his designs for merchant galleys and war galleons are still the most duplicated in the kingdoms.

Master Shipwright	A master class shipbuilder, a highly sought after craftsman. Many live in Klaive and Wellison. To become a master shipwright, one must be able to read and write (rare skills in many parts of the kingdoms) and must prove oneself as a ship architect, designing and building multisailed vessels under the watchful eye of a current master shipwright.
Shipwright	A builder of ships. Klaive is the primary shipbuilding port in Great Kingdom. Wellison is Sever's shipbuilding port.
Shipper	An apprentice shipwright.

Smiths, Weaponsmiths & Armorsmiths

Every village and city throughout the kingdoms has one thing in common: Each has a blacksmith and that blacksmith is one of the most highly respected members of the community. It takes a certain kind of man (or woman) to pound steel, shape it against its will, and create the tools, weapons, and armor that are needed throughout the lands.

Master Smith	A master class smith, often working at garrisons and kingdom outposts. Master weaponsmiths and master armorsmiths specialize in the making of finely crafted weapons and armor respectively. The road to becoming a master smith is one of the longest in all the kingdom trades, especially for weapon and armor smiths. Master smiths earn their title by creating durable goods of fine quality. Claim the title too early, and a smith could end up with the sharp end of blade between the eyes.
Smith	A forger of steel and other metals, a maker of weapons and armor. Weaponsmiths and armorsmiths are specialists in the making of weapons and armor respectively.
Ironer	An apprentice smith.

Stonecutters

Master stonecutters are the true wizards of the land. They use stones cut from mountains, dug from quarries, or shaped in kilns to build the unyielding structures needed to protect kingdomers from natural disasters and attack, to traverse rivers without having to find a ford, and to collect water from far-away places. Master stonecutters are the architects of castles, bridges, aqueducts, and roads. Kings, lords, ladies, and commoners alike commission their services.

Master Stonecutter	A master class stone and brick mason. To become a master stonecutter, a stonecutter must ply his trade for many years, honing his skills until he is recognized as the best of the best. As with smiths, it is a long road to becoming a master stonecutter, but the good news is that stonecutters often get to pave their own road through life.
Stonecutter	A journeyman class stone and brick mason. Stonecutters know how to cut and shape stones, how to make and kiln brick, and how to mix quicklime.
Stoner	An apprentice mason.

Tanners

Away from the great cities of the Kingdoms where silk and cloth abound, the master tanner sets the fashion trend of the day with fur and leather. Take a tanner enough rabbit pelts, come back when it's time, and you'll have a coat. But being a tanner isn't only about making clothes. Tanners make other goods, such as leatherskin canoes, covers for wagons, and padded leather suits for protection in the wilds.

Master Tanner	A master class tanner. To become a master tanner requires great skill. A tanner must be able to fashion many different types of goods using wits and the animal skins supplied. Sometimes a tanner must make do with what's available, fashioning the needed item as much with faith as with anything else.
Tanner	A tanner of animal skins, a maker of leather goods.
Hidesman	An apprentice tanner.

Woodworkers

Because skills and preferences vary so greatly, woodworkers are some of the most misunderstood tradesmen in the whole of the kingdoms. Some woodworkers build structures: bridges, houses, and mills. Some prefer wagons, coaches, and carriages. Others become specialists, crafting small trade goods.

Master Woodworker	A master class woodworker. Master woodworkers often work with master stonecutters on construction projects, and their craft shows clearly in many structures, even those that are mostly of stone. To become a master woodworker, one must become the best at his craft and work hard to make a name for himself in his chosen area of woodworking.
Woodworker	A craftsman who works with wood and has passed an apprenticeship.
Wooder	An apprentice woodworker.

Review Questions for Discussion

Review Questions for Discussion: Chapters 1-2

1. Why is Princess Adrina sad at the beginning of the story? (She's maturing and has more responsibilities. Her siblings are grown and have moved away. Now it's her time to learn her heritage and become a lady. Her mother died and she feels lonely.)

2. Why is it important that Vilmos learn how to listen carefully to others? (His father is the village Counselor and he might someday take his father's place. Listening is an important skill for a counselor because if he doesn't pay close attention he may give the wrong advice to those seeking his help.)

3. What does Seth learn from Queen Mother as they walk to Sanctuary's High Hall that startles him? (The queen intends to break the link between them. She says that times are changing—their people have lived in fear of repeating the past and only succeeded in repeating it. Seth is afraid for her safety.)

4. Why does King Andrew tell Princess Adrina "Only so, dear Adrina. Only so," and what does he mean? (Adrina is almost late to dinner and he's telling her this politely. At the same time, he watches the reactions of the honored guests at his table.)

5. What's so important about the messenger's arrival during the evening meal? (The messenger has urgent news for the king. This interrupts the meal and Adrina sees this as a sign of the coming change the old woman told her of.)

6. Why is Queen Mother upset when she talks with Brother Liyan? (Because he questions her intention to send Seth on a journey to the lands of men. This changes her mood from bright to somber, and reminds her of the things she was trying to forget.)

7. What happens when Vilmos meets the bear in the forest? (He gets scared and pees his pants. He's afraid the bear will attack him. When it does, something strange happens. The bear vanishes and Vilmos smells burning hair, flesh, and wood. Then Vilmos realizes he used his magic—he had conjured the blue flames.

8. What does Seth mean by these statements: Galan had the insatiable curiosity of a preborn child. She held the same view of looking at the world. She saw things as flashes of color and feelings. Only Galan would ask what he found most odd about them [men]. (He thinks that Galan has a unique way of looking at the world. She is curious about everyone and everything. She must also openly express her feelings and thoughts about what she sees and experiences. In a society that seems as closed as that of the Elven Brotherhood, her way of thinking must be very unique indeed.)

Review Questions for Discussion: Chapters 3-4

1. Why does Lady Isador tell Princess Adrina "Down, down, down dear. No wonder that hem looked all wrong. Mustn't stand on tiptoes."? (Lady Isador is trying to hem Adrina's dress, but Adrina isn't standing still. She's anxious because she heard the palace heralds and because she thinks another messenger has arrived. The last message seems to have been from King Charles of Sever, and, according to rumors, something was terribly wrong.)

2. Seth feels helpless as he waits in the antechamber. He considers eavesdropping. Do you think he should have? Would you have eavesdropped if you were Seth and could read others' thoughts? (Seth is waiting to find out what's going to happen. He might not know for certain what Queen Mother plans, but he suspects, and Galan also tells him that she is afraid for him. This gives him a lot to think about.)

3. Why are Vilmos' parents so frightened when he tells what happened with the bear? (Magic use is forbidden, at least for them. They think magic is bad and that something bad will happen if people find out that Vilmos can use magic.

4. Why does Brother Liyan think Seth is afraid of leaving? (Seth had never traveled beyond the city or the sanctuary of the elves. Seth had never been out into the world, and Brother Liyan thinks that may be the one thing Seth is afraid of. Seth is also confused because he has strong feelings for Galan but he has never told her. Seth thinks his feelings are wrong, but Brother Liyan tells him the feelings are as natural as wind.)

5. Why do you think Emel calls Adrina a "fair-weather friend"? (Something happened and Adrina let Emel take the blame for it. Because of that, Emel was sent away for a long time to High Road Garrison, and, after he returned, Adrina didn't talk to him.)

6. Why does Chancellor Yi wake up King Andrew in the middle of the night? (Keeper Martin, head of all the Keepers of the Lore, arrives unexpectedly in the night. Keeper Martin says it is an urgent matter for the king.)

7. Did Captain Brodst really attack Adrina or was it a misunderstanding? Summarize what happened and why. (It was a misunderstanding. Adrina fell asleep in the hallway and when Captain Brodst woke her up, she started screaming. Things got worse when Lady Isador came to Adrina's rescue and eventually guards are surrounding the captain.)

8. What does Adrina take from Emel that prevents him from doing his duties, and why? (Adrina takes the harness he needs and won't give it back. She wants to go with Emel and thinks that he'll let her if she persists.)

9. Why do you think Emel's horse is called Ebony Lightning, and why do you think the king gave the horse to him? (Emel's horse is black and fast. He is proud of the horse, so he called it Ebony Lightning. The book mentions again his going to High Road Garrison during the past winter and spring. Since he was given the horse when he returned, the king might know the truth about what happened that caused Emel to be sent away. Or the horse might have been given for some other reason, such as to ensure that Emel stayed away from Adrina.

Teacher's Classroom Guide   Robert Stanek's Ruin Mist

Review Questions for Discussion: Chapters 5-6

1. Does Vilmos like or dislike doing "housework"? Explain. (Vilmos likes to help his mother, but he thinks "housework" is a "woman's chore," which are probably his father's words. His mother calls it "honest work" though, and he does feel good when he helps his mother.)

2. What is the secret place Vilmos visits in his dreams, and what is so wrong about going there? (He visits a valley and becomes an eagle. He uses magic; something a voice tells him is "non-corporeal stasis, " an out of body experience. It is wrong because he is using magic and he's not supposed to, but also because the voice tells him that when he's in the valley any spirit can enter his body.)

3. What happens when Vilmos confronts the stranger and tells him to show himself? (Vilmos sees a frail and weak old man. He imagines that a heavy wind could blow the man away, and then a wind starts to blow. The wind doesn't affect the old man, but it nearly kills Vilmos by almost blowing him over a ledge.)

4. Why does Adrina start to worry about Emel when she hears the trumpets sounding? (Emel taught her what the trumpet calls meant, so she knew it was a call to arms. Since Emel was out in the fields beyond Imtal, she was worried about his safety.)

5. Why do you think Adrina almost runs to Emel when he returns, but then looks away? (She likes Emel, but she's not supposed to. Emel might like her too. When their eyes meet, maybe she looks away because she's afraid of following her true feelings, or maybe because Emel says Adrina's attendant is pretty.)

6. What happened to Ridemaster Gabrylle out Braddabaggon Way and why is it funny? (A lowland cat startles the ridemaster's horse. He falls and breaks his leg, which isn't funny, but the way Emel tells the story makes it funny. It's funny too because of the young ridesman, who is so scared after seeing the cat that they have to pry the sword out of his hand.

7. What does Lady Isador mean when she says, "Odd though it is, all I want to do now is go home. You see, home is the place you try so very hard to get away from, only to miss dearly when you are gone." (She's trying to tell Adrina that when she was young all she wanted to do was get away from home too, but now, in a way, she wishes she could go home. She's trying to explain to Adrina that she might think she wants to get away from home now, but if she does she might then realize what she had and miss it.)

8. Why does Adrina say she doesn't want her life decided for her? (She doesn't want to be promised in marriage like her sisters. Her sister Calyin was promised in marriage to Lord Serant of the Territories. Her father also tried to promise her sister Midori in marriage to King Jarom.)

9. Why does King Andrew say he is beyond healing and that he sees pain in Adrina's eyes? (The queen passed away and he hasn't come to terms with her death yet. He thinks the pain is so deep that he can never heal, and it makes him sad when he sees this sadness in Adrina's eyes. He hopes that when she leaves home on her travels she will finally heal.)

Review Questions for Discussion: Chapters 7-8

1. Who is waiting for Vilmos when he returns from the strange encounter in the valley, and what happens afterward? (His tutor, Midori, is waiting for him. He discovers that what happened was real. Midori uses a magic stone to heal his hands, but can't heal the wounds on his shoulders.)

2. Where does Midori take Vilmos and why does he think he won't be going home again? (Midori leads Vilmos away from danger. She takes him to meet Xith, someone she says is a friend and who might be a gnome.)

3. Why does Xith say, "History belongs to the teller and is only as reliable as the teller's recollection of it."? (Because different people can see things differently, or they might remember something differently than someone else.)

4. Why does Emel ride away from Adrina? (She isn't treating him fairly, and instead of giving him a straight answer to his question, she plays with him. She feels poorly afterward for doing that.)

5. Why are soldiers staring at Adrina when she goes to the edge of the stream? (She did a most unlady-like thing, she washed in the stream and then took her boots off and dangled her toes in the water. A long time ago, it wasn't proper for a lady, especially a princess, to do such a thing in public, and probably the soldiers had never seen someone like Adrina do such a thing.)

6. What happens when Emel and Adrina ride away from the column? Do you think that was a smart thing to do given the circumstances? (Adrina chases after Emel and they begin to race. When Emel grabs the reins of Adrina's horse, she falls into the mud. Then she pulls him into the mud and they throw mud at each other.)

7. Who do Adrina and Emel meet in the forest, and what do they learn? (They meet a strange group of travelers. A mysterious lady in this group warns them and tells them about the change taking place.)

8. Who is Myrial, and why does the lady ask Adrina about her? (The lady is making a point that Adrina has lost touch with the people of her realm and that she doesn't even know the names of those who serve and take care of her. She tells her this because she wants her to open her eyes to the world around her.)

Teacher's Classroom Guide	Robert Stanek's Ruin Mist

Review Questions for Discussion: Chapters 9-10

1. Why does Seth decide to rely on Captain Cagan when the elves are ambushed? (Seth doesn't know the world or the sea. Cagan does, however. Cagan is a strong sailor and surely knows better than Seth how to get through the blockade. Seth trusts Cagan.)

2. What does it mean to guide a ship into the head of a gull and why did Cagan do that? (Cagan turned the ship to get maximum benefit from the winds. The wind filled the sails and helped the Lady L outpace the other ships.)

3. Why does Cagan say, "It is only us at the last."? (Because only a few survived the ambush, and he and Seth were among the survivors.)

4. How does Vilmos discover he won't be going home? Would you trust Xith like Vilmos does? (Xith tells Vilmos that he knew his real birth mother and that he is the one who placed Vilmos with Lillath and her husband. Xith tells Vilmos that he won't be going home because the time the shaman was waiting for had come.)

5. What happens when Vilmos learns that his "father" really loved him? (Vilmos cries. He thought his father was punishing him to be mean, but his father was actually trying to protect him. His father didn't want Vilmos to have to go away as Xith foretold.)

6. Where is Xith taking Vilmos, and what hints does Vilmos give that his perception about this place is different than Xith's or others who may live in this place? (Xith is taking Vilmos to the Alder's Kingdom, also called Great Kingdom. At first Vilmos says that nothing is north, and Xith answers that that is what he has been told. Vilmos also mentions hearing strange tales about the Borderlands.)

7. What do you think Xith means when he says, "There is no simple path to follow," and what is he trying to teach Vilmos? (Xith may be trying to teach Vilmos patience, but he also wants Vilmos to learn to follow through on his actions. He wants Vilmos to learn that when you start something, you should finish it.)

8. What does Xith reveal about magic and Vilmos' dreams? (Xith tells Vilmos that the dreams are the playing out of good and evil, and that many would-be mages in the past succumbed to the dark magic. He goes on to say that a world without magic isn't safe. Although magic is a part of the story that's fantasy, it's analogous to saying how terrible it would be to live in a world without hopes and dreams.)

Teacher's Classroom Guide   Robert Stanek's Ruin Mist

Review Questions for Discussion: Chapters 11-12

1. What decision is weighing heavily on Adrina's thoughts as she rides through Mellack Proper? (She wants to tell someone besides Emel about the encounter with the mysterious lady in the forest. However, she isn't sure if that's a good idea, and she's not sure who to tell.)

2. Who does Adrina decide to tell about her secret and why? (Adrina is troubled by the secret she has been keeping from everyone. She has been thinking of telling Father Jacob, Keeper Martin, or Captain Brodst. Emel says Keeper Martin is the wisest man in the kingdom, so she finally decides to tell him.)

3. What does Adrina mean when she thinks that Keeper Martin is "a man who preferred his records and his tomes to human companionship." Do you know anyone like this? (Keeper Martin is a scholar. He's a bit bookish, and is probably more comfortable with his books and studies than he is with people.)

4. Why does Emel avoid Adrina after they make camp in Ispeth? (His father has ordered him to go south with a detachment to Quashan'. He is obviously worried about what might happen to Adrina while he is away, and that is upsetting him.)

5. Why do you think Adrina chases after Emel when he goes away, but then tells him to give her regards to her brother? (She doesn't want Emel to go. She is sad because he is leaving. She wants to tell him how she really feels about him, but then she can't follow through and instead says what is safe.)

6. What happens when Vilmos and Xith enter Vangar Forest? (Something starts to follow them. They try to get away but it seems they are being led into a trap. Vilmos and Xith get separated for a time. Later Vilmos finds out that the beasts chasing them are called Wolmerrelle.)

7. Why do you think the author calls these creatures Wolmerrelle and what do you know about them? (When Vilmos faces one of the Wolmerrelle, he sees a creature with two heads and two mouths filled with canine fangs. Xith hints that these creatures are the result of beasts from different realms mating. Perhaps these creatures are part wolf and part something else.)

8. What do you think will happen to Vilmos if he returns to Vangar Forest? (The Wolmerrelle will be waiting for him, and they will catch him—that's what Vilmos thinks anyway.)

Review Questions for Discussion: Chapters 13-14

1. What does the author mean when he says Captain Brodst has a customary frown? (Captain Brodst doesn't smile. It may be that he is an unhappy person or that he is someone who worries about things.)

2. Why does Adrina feel uneasy when she rides through the rolling hills toward the Bottoms? (It's raining again and everyone is wet. The mires have a dark history, and Adrina is worried about what waits for them ahead.)

3. What do you think caused Adrina to feel unseen hands grabbing for her? Have you ever felt like that? (She's afraid of the mires. It's foggy and hard to see. The air is cold and so is she. Her imagination begins to take over her thoughts. She begins to feel and see things that aren't there.)

4. What happens to Adrina when she lets her fears take over? (Her actions become confused. She sends mixed signals to her horse. As a result, the horse falters on the side of the road and both the horse and the rider fall. Adrina ends up under water with the horse on top of her.)

5. Why does Xith feel he must make Vilmos face his fears? (He thinks it will prepare Vilmos for what he must face in the future, and that someday Vilmos will be out of places to run to.)

6. The Great Book of Sever describes the lands to the north as a place of desolation. Why do you think it's important that Vilmos learn the truth about the outside lands? (Vilmos is finding that there is a whole world beyond Sever's borders. He is learning that not everything you read is the truth, or that perhaps the world has changed since the Great Book was first written. Perhaps it will lead him to question other things written in the Great Book, and to learn the truth about those things himself.)

7. When Vilmos sees the innkeeper, what does he assume and later learn? (From the description it seems Vilmos doesn't think highly of the innkeeper. He thinks of him as fat and as having an unpleasant odor. Later he is surprised to find that the innkeeper and Xith are friends, and that the innkeeper is a wonderful cook. His opinion of the innkeeper quickly changes and he may have learned that it is important not to judge people without getting to know them first.)

8. When Vilmos recalls what the Great Book says about the Alder Kingdom and the Race Wars, what do you think is the point of the lesson that he remembers? (Whole peoples and nations perished during the war, and the once great kingdoms of the north disappeared. Lycya was swallowed by the desert. The elves were washed into the sea. North Reach and the clans were buried in snow. Only the Alder Kingdom survived, and according to the Great Book, they did this by signing a treaty with the southern kingdoms.)

Review Questions for Discussion: Chapters 15-16

1. What happened to Seth and his companions, and who survived the initial disaster? (Their ships sank and almost everyone perished. Seth, Bryan, Everelle, and Galan survived.)

2. What does Seth do to help ensure the safety of his friends? What would you have done if you were him? (Seth puts others before himself. He binds his companions' wounds first because they can't help themselves. He rations the supplies, gives others what little water they have. He tries to shield them from the sun and also to catch fish to feed them.)

3. Chapter 16 is titled "Return." What event does that hint at? (Adrina is near death after falling from her horse and getting crushed beneath it. The title hints at her return from unconsciousness.)

4. Why didn't Father Jacob perform mouth-to-mouth resuscitation on Adrina when she was pulled from the water? (Mouth-to-mouth resuscitation is a life-saving technique used to help restore breathing to someone who isn't breathing. Father Jacob probably didn't know this technique as it is unique to our time and not his own. Had Father Jacob known about this technique, he surely would have performed it.)

5. What do you think will happen next to Seth, Adrina, Vilmos, and their friends? (While *The Kingdoms & the Elves of the Reaches II* provides the answers, there is certainly a lot to think about based on what readers already know. Seth will have to find a way to survive on the open sea. Adrina will reach Alderan and find out what is happening to Great Kingdom. Vilmos will continue his journey north with Xith and will certainly reach Great Kingdom soon.)

Quizzes

Teacher's Classroom Guide   Robert Stanek's Ruin Mist

Quiz!: Chapters 1-2

1. Why is Princess Adrina sad at the beginning of the story?
_____
_____

2. Why is it important that Vilmos learn how to listen carefully to others?
_____
_____

3. What does Seth learn from Queen Mother as they walk to Sanctuary's High Hall that startles him?
_____
_____

4. Why does King Andrew tell Princess Adrina "Only so, dear Adrina. Only so," and what does he mean?
_____
_____

5. What's so important about the messenger's arrival during the evening meal?
_____
_____

6. Why is Queen Mother upset when she talks with Brother Liyan?
_____
_____

7. What happens when Vilmos meets the bear in the forest?
_____
_____

8. What does Seth mean by these statements: Galan had the insatiable curiosity of a preborn child. She held the same view of looking at the world. She saw things as flashes of color and feelings. Only Galan would ask what he found most odd about them [men].
_____
_____

Teacher's Classroom Guide　　　　　　　　　　　　　　　Robert Stanek's Ruin Mist

Quiz!: Chapters 3-4

1. Why does Lady Isador tell Princess Adrina "Down, down, down dear. No wonder that hem looked all wrong. Mustn't stand on tiptoes."?

2. Seth feels helpless as he waits in the antechamber. He considers eavesdropping. Do you think he should have? Would you have eavesdropped if you were Seth?

3. Why are Vilmos' parents so frightened when he tells what happened with the bear?

4. Why does Brother Liyan think Seth is afraid of leaving?

5. Why do you think Emel calls Adrina a "fair-weather friend"?

6. Why does Chancellor Yi wake up King Andrew in the middle of the night?

7. Did Captain Brodst really attack Adrina or was it a misunderstanding? Summarize what happened and why.

8. What does Adrina take from Emel that prevents him from doing his duties, and why?

9. Why do you think Emel's horse is called Ebony Lightning, and why do you think the king gave the horse to him?

Teacher's Classroom Guide Robert Stanek's Ruin Mist

Quiz!: Chapters 5-6

1. Does Vilmos like or dislike doing "housework"? Explain.

2. What's the secret place Vilmos visits in his dreams? What's so wrong about going there?

3. What happens when Vilmos confronts the stranger and tells him to show himself?

4. Why does Adrina start to worry about Emel when she hears the trumpets sounding?

5. Why do you think Adrina almost runs to Emel when he returns, but then looks away?

6. What happened to Ridemaster Gabrylle out Braddabaggon Way and why is it funny?

7. What does Lady Isador mean when she says, "Odd though it is, all I want to do now is go home. You see, home is the place you try so very hard to get away from, only to miss dearly when you are gone."

8. Why does Adrina say she doesn't want her life decided for her?

9. Why does King Andrew say he is beyond healing, and that he sees pain in Adrina's eyes?

Teacher's Classroom Guide　　　　　　　　　　　　　Robert Stanek's Ruin Mist

Quiz!: Chapters 7-8

1. Who is waiting for Vilmos when he returns from the strange encounter in the valley, and what happens afterward?
_____
_____

2. Where does Midori take Vilmos, and why does he think he won't be going home again?
_____
_____

3. Why does Xith say, "History belongs to the teller and is only as reliable as the teller's recollection of it."?
_____
_____

4. Why does Emel ride away from Adrina?
_____
_____

5. Why are soldiers staring at Adrina when she goes to the edge of the stream?
_____
_____

6. What happens when Emel and Adrina ride away from the column? Do you think that was a smart thing to do given the circumstances?
_____
_____

7. Who do Adrina and Emel meet in the forest, and what do they learn?
_____
_____

8. Who is Myrial, and why does the lady ask Adrina about her?
_____
_____

Teacher's Classroom Guide   Robert Stanek's Ruin Mist

Quiz!: Chapters 9-10

1. Why does Seth decide to rely on Captain Cagan when the elves are ambushed?
_____
_____

2. What does it mean to guide a ship into the head of a gull, and why did Cagan do that?
_____
_____

3. Why does Cagan say, "It is only us at the last."?
_____
_____

4. How does Vilmos discover he won't be going home? Would you trust Xith like Vilmos does?
_____
_____

5. What happens when Vilmos learns that his "father" really loved him?
_____
_____

6. Where is Xith taking Vilmos, and what hints does Vilmos give that his perception about this place is different than Xith's or others who may live in this place?
_____
_____

7. What do you think Xith means when he says, "There is no simple path to follow," and what is he trying to teach Vilmos?
_____
_____

8. What does Xith reveal about magic and Vilmos' dreams?
_____
_____

Teacher's Classroom Guide   Robert Stanek's Ruin Mist

Quiz!: Chapters 11-12

1. What decision is weighing heavily on Adrina's thoughts as she rides through Mellack Proper?
___
___

2. Who does Adrina decide to tell about her secret and why?
___
___

3. What does Adrina mean when she thinks that Keeper Martin is "a man who preferred his records and his tomes to human companionship." Do you know anyone like this?
___
___

4. Why does Emel avoid Adrina after they make camp in Ispeth?
___
___

5. Why do you think Adrina chases after Emel when he goes away, but then tells him to give her regards to her brother?
___
___

6. What happens when Vilmos and Xith enter Vangar Forest?
___
___

7. Why do you think the author calls these creatures Wolmerrelle, and what do you know about them?
___
___

8. What do you think will happen to Vilmos if he returns to Vangar Forest?
___
___

Teacher's Classroom Guide   Robert Stanek's Ruin Mist

Quiz!: Chapters 13-14

1. What does the author mean when he says Captain Brodst has a customary frown?
_____
_____

2. Why does Adrina feel uneasy when she rides through the rolling hills toward the Bottoms?
_____
_____

3. What do you think caused Adrina to feel unseen hands grabbing for her? Have you ever felt like that?
_____
_____

4. What happens to Adrina when she lets her fears take over?
_____
_____

5. Why does Xith feel he must make Vilmos face his fears?
_____
_____

6. The Great Book of Sever describes the lands to the north as a place of desolation. Why do you think it's important that Vilmos learn the truth about the outside lands?
_____
_____

7. When Vilmos sees the innkeeper, what does he assume and later learn?
_____
_____

8. When Vilmos recalls what the Great Book says about the Alder Kingdom and the Race Wars, what do you think is the point of the lesson that he remembers?
_____
_____

Teacher's Classroom Guide   Robert Stanek's Ruin Mist

Quiz!: Chapters 15-16

1. What happened to Seth and his companions, and who survived the initial disaster?
_____
_____

2. What does Seth do to help ensure the safety of his friends? What would you have done if you were him?
_____
_____
_____

3. Chapter 16 is titled "Return." What event does that hint at?
_____
_____
_____

4. Why didn't Father Jacob perform mouth-to-mouth resuscitation on Adrina when she was pulled from the water?
_____
_____

5. What do you think will happen next to Seth, Adrina, Vilmos, and their friends?
_____
_____
_____
_____
_____
_____
_____
_____
_____
_____

Post-Reading Activities

Teacher's Classroom Guide — Robert Stanek's Ruin Mist

Sorrow & Grief

Princess Adrina is sad because her mother passed away some years ago. Her mother's death was simply too much for her, and it doesn't seem that she has anyone to turn to for help. This great sadness changes her view of everything she sees and experiences.

At some time in our life all of us might experience sorrow and grief. We might not know what to do. We might not admit that we are sad and that we need help because we are too proud or too afraid. If we don't deal with grief, our personalities might change. Instead of being fun and outgoing, we might become quiet and reserved.

Has anything every happened to you that made you very sad? What did you do?

_____
_____
_____

If you were Princess Adrina, what would you do differently? Who would you turn to for help?

_____
_____
_____

Later in the story, we find out that King Andrew, Adrina's father, is just as sad as she is. Why do you think they didn't turn to each other for help?

_____
_____
_____

What would you do if you knew a grown-up that was so sad and needed help but didn't know how to ask for it?

_____
_____
_____
_____

Responsibilities

Vilmos is impatient a lot of the time. He wants to do and experience things, to have fun, to go and run through the woods. But he can't always do what he wants because he has responsibilities. As a Counselor's son, listening is an important skill for him to learn because if he doesn't pay close attention he might give the wrong advice to someone who needs his help.

At some time all of us act like Vilmos. We don't want to be responsible. We don't want to listen or do the things we should. We might lie when we are asked about what we've done. If someone tells on us, we might try to get back at them or tease them, which isn't the right thing to do.

Have you ever done anything that you knew was wrong, or skipped doing homework or household chores? Why?

_____

_____

What happened when your parents, friends, or teachers found out about what you did? How did that make you feel?

_____

_____

Did you ever try to get back at someone who told the truth about something bad you did? Describe the situation, and then put yourself in the other person's place and consider how it made them feel.

_____

_____

_____

Why do you think listening and doing what is right is so important? Would you want to live in a world where everyone broke the rules?

_____

_____

_____

Eavesdropping

When Seth is waiting outside High Hall, he is tempted to eavesdrop. He doesn't know for certain what's happening, and what Galan has told him has made him afraid of what's going to happen.

This gives Seth a lot to think about, but in the end he doesn't eavesdrop on that conversation. For him, it was a conscious, moral decision. He felt that it was wrong to eavesdrop in that situation.

Do you think Seth made the right decision? Why or why not?

_____
_____
_____

If you remember the story, Galan did eavesdrop on an earlier conversation. That's how she found out something that she wasn't supposed to know, and why she was afraid for Seth. Do you think what Galan did was wrong? Was she wrong to warn Seth?

_____
_____
_____

Have you ever wanted to listen in on someone else's conversation even though you knew you probably shouldn't? Did you? Why or why not?

_____
_____
_____

If someone told you a secret and then you told someone else that secret, do you think that's just as bad as eavesdropping when you know you're not supposed to? What if it was a bad secret that someone should know about?

_____
_____
_____

Friendship & Loyalty

Princess Adrina and Emel have a very complicated friendship. Emel thinks of Adrina as a "fair-weather friend" and perhaps she is, but perhaps there is something more to their friendship than either will admit. In their past together, Adrina let Emel take the blame for something and it resulted in him being sent away for a long time to High Road Garrison.

What do you think it means to be a friend to someone?
___
___
___

Why do you think Emel took the blame for something Adrina did?
___
___
___

Would you take the blame for something your friend did? Why or why not?
___
___
___

If you asked your friends to describe the type of friend you are, what do you think they would say about you?
___
___
___

Why do you think it is so important to have friends and to make friends with those who might not have friends?
___
___
___

Perceptions & Misconceptions

Perceptions and, more specifically, ill-conceived perceptions about what the characters think of things they see and experience play an important part in the story. Adrina doesn't really see what's around her. She thinks everything is dead and gray, and the mysterious lady of the forest tries to open her eyes to the real world around her.

Vilmos has a secret place he likes to visit. He goes there because he feels safe. We would all probably like to have a secret place that we could go to sometimes, but, like Vilmos, we might find that that secret place isn't what we think it is. His secret place turns out to be a real place—a dangerous place.

Seth has tremendous skills as a warrior and as an intellectual, yet he has no worldly experience. He is afraid of change, and he doesn't want to leave his home. Like Vilmos, he also has misconceptions about what the outside world is like.

Work in groups to decide ways in which misconceptions affected the characters in the story. Discuss how their views might be different if they didn't have these misconceptions. Discuss misconceptions that you might have and what you could do to change them. Be ready to share your discussion with the class.

Write down your ideas.

_____
_____
_____
_____
_____
_____
_____
_____
_____
_____
_____

Write a Journal!

Write a journal entry from either the point of view of Adrina or Vilmos describing their thoughts pertaining to the other character. Be creative, in depth, and descriptive in your writing.

What's the Main Idea?

Select four chapters from the book and describe why you think the author named the titles the way he did. Use specific examples from the book to explain your answer. Be as detailed as possible.

Be the Character!

Pick Vilmos, Adrina, Seth, Emel, or Xith. Imagine they are living in your world. Then pick a place where they will live in your world and describe how they would feel and also what they would think, see, and hear. Try to describe everyday objects as if you do not know what they are. For example, a car could be described as a shiny metal monster as opposed to just calling it a car. Pick a creative style to mirror the character's feelings and thoughts.

_____
_____
_____
_____
_____
_____
_____
_____
_____
_____
_____
_____
_____
_____
_____
_____
_____
_____
_____
_____
_____
_____

What's in a Personality?

Compare and contrast the personalities of Vilmos and Adrina. Write about their personalities as well as physical attributes. Expand upon your thoughts and create an interesting and factual paper.

Explore Ruin Mist (English)

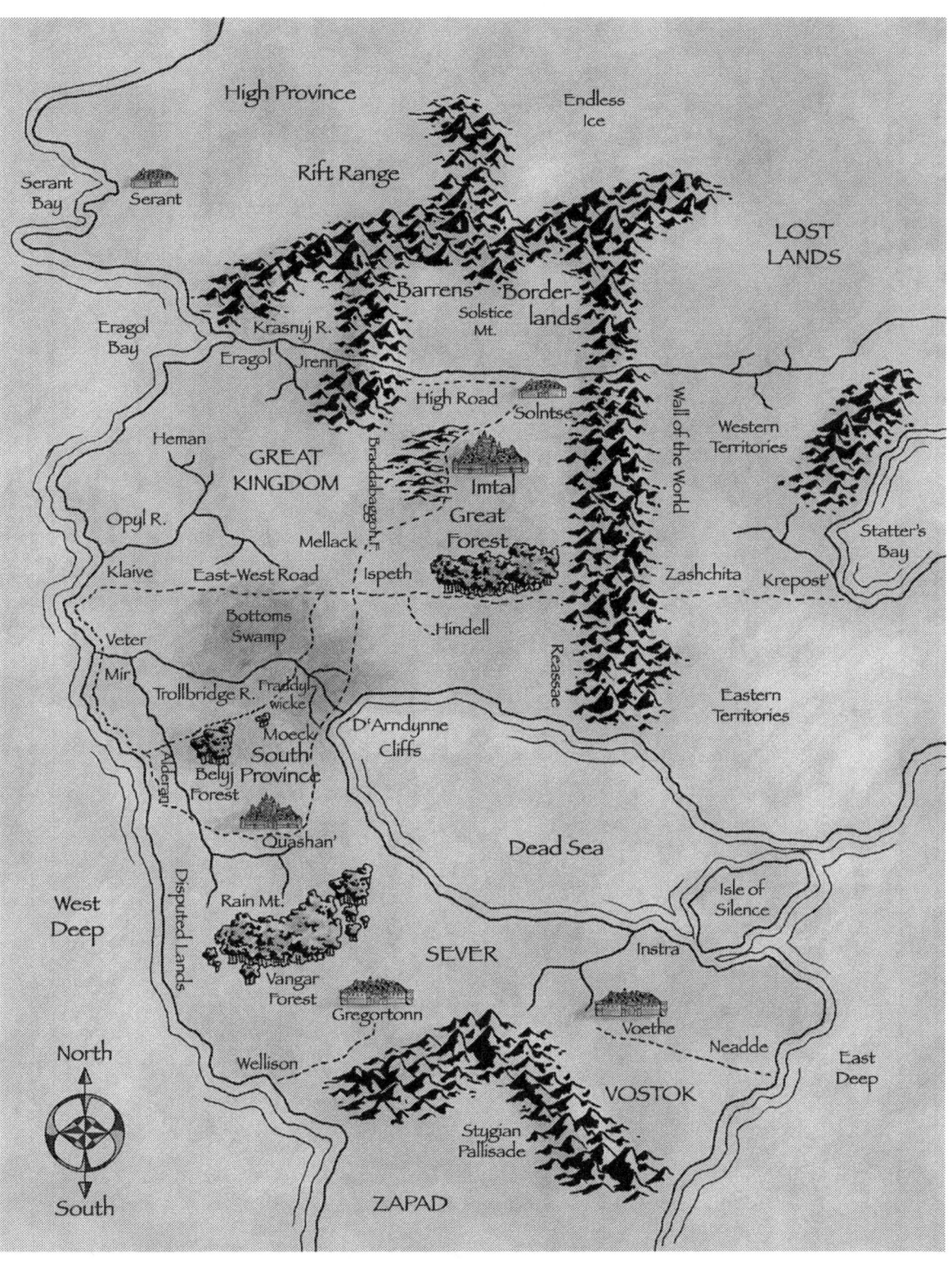

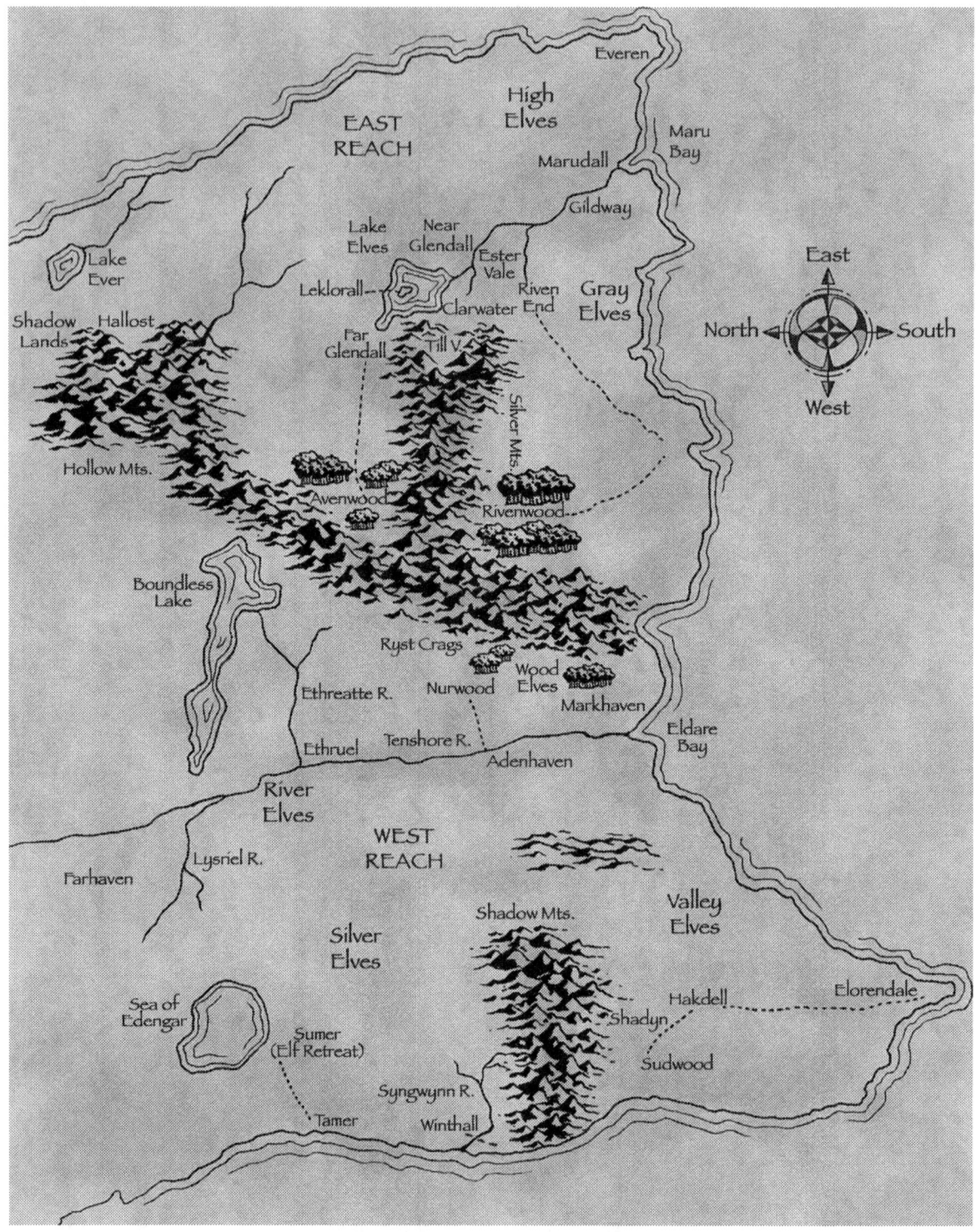

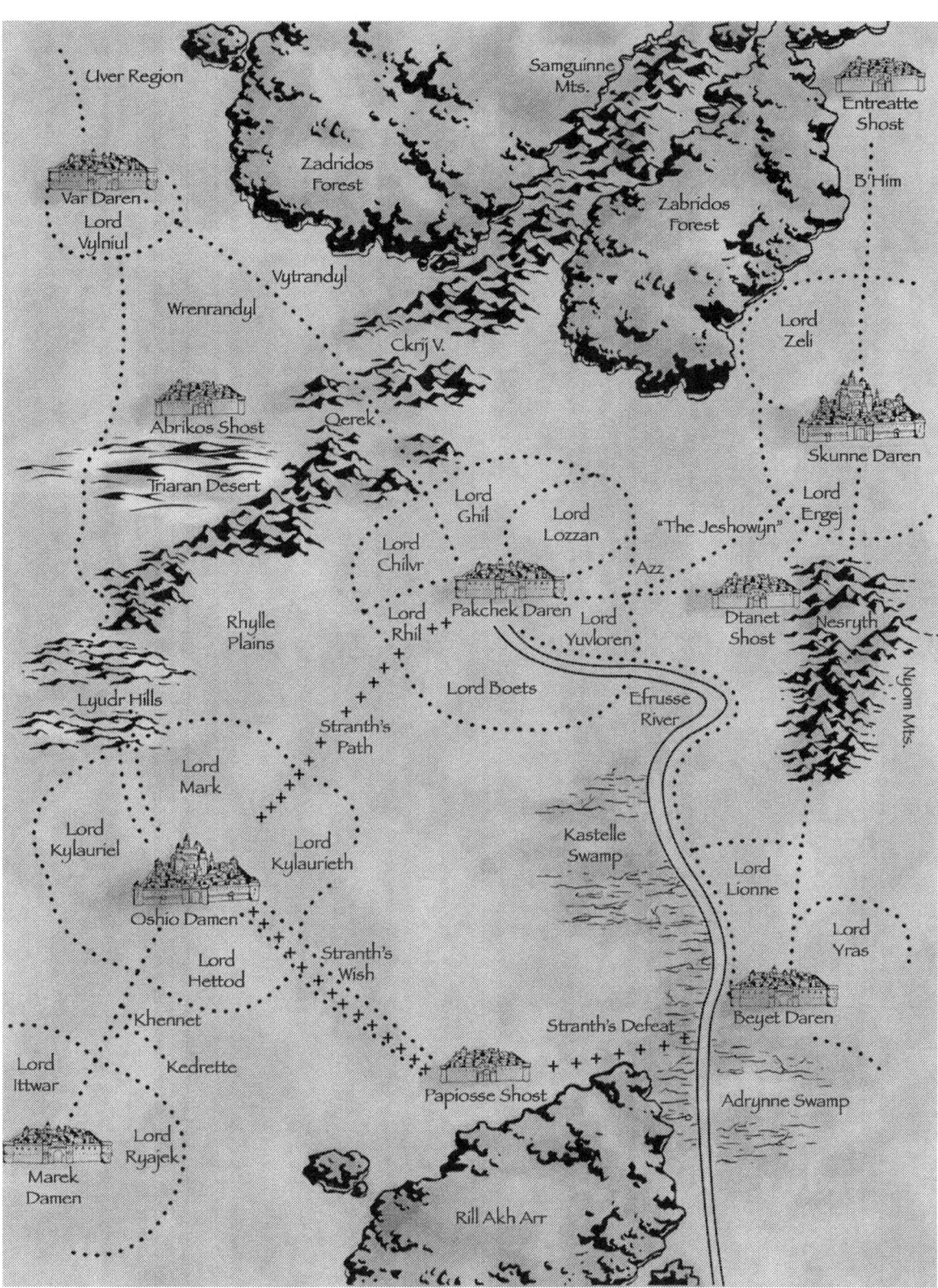

Explore Ruin Mist
(Spanish)

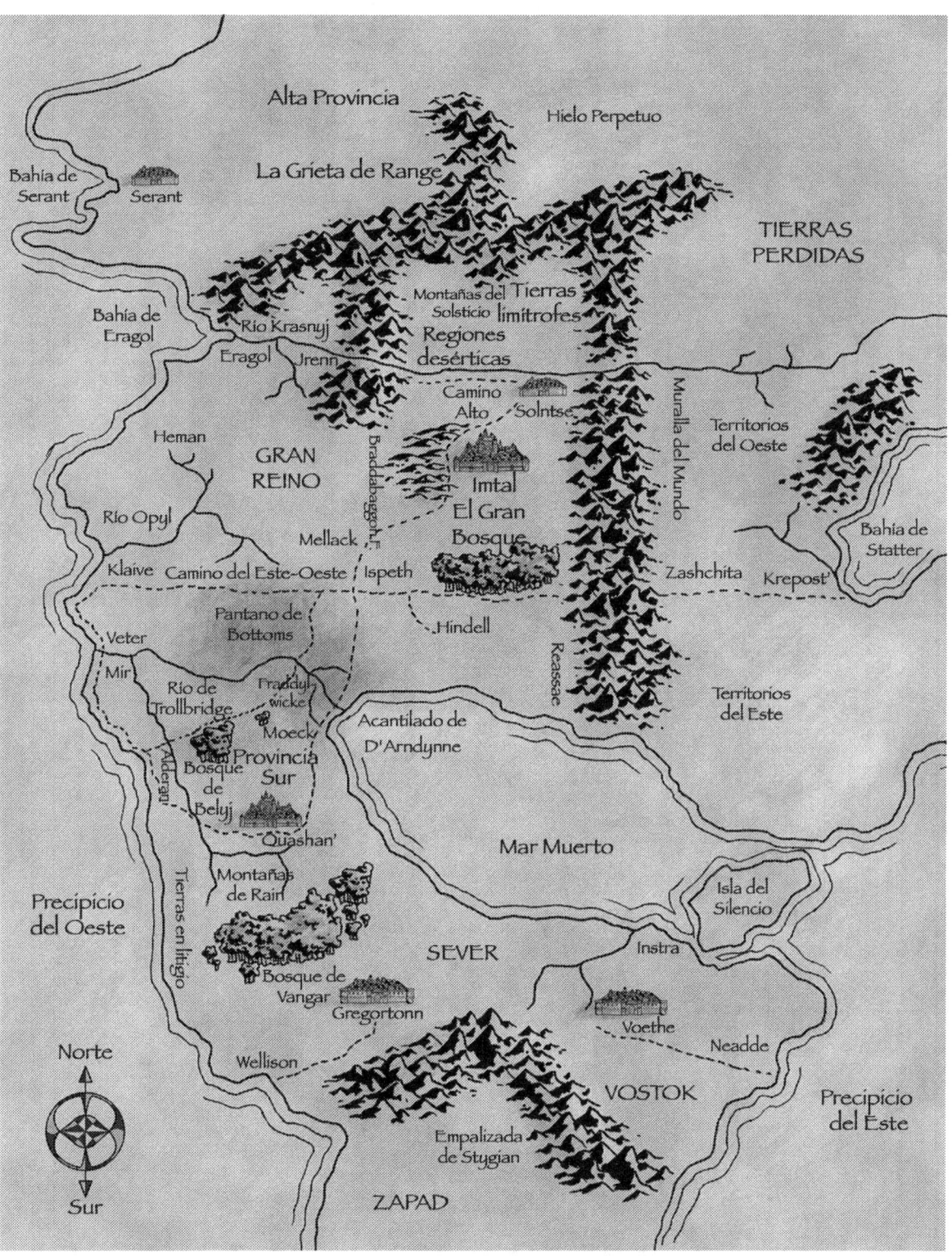

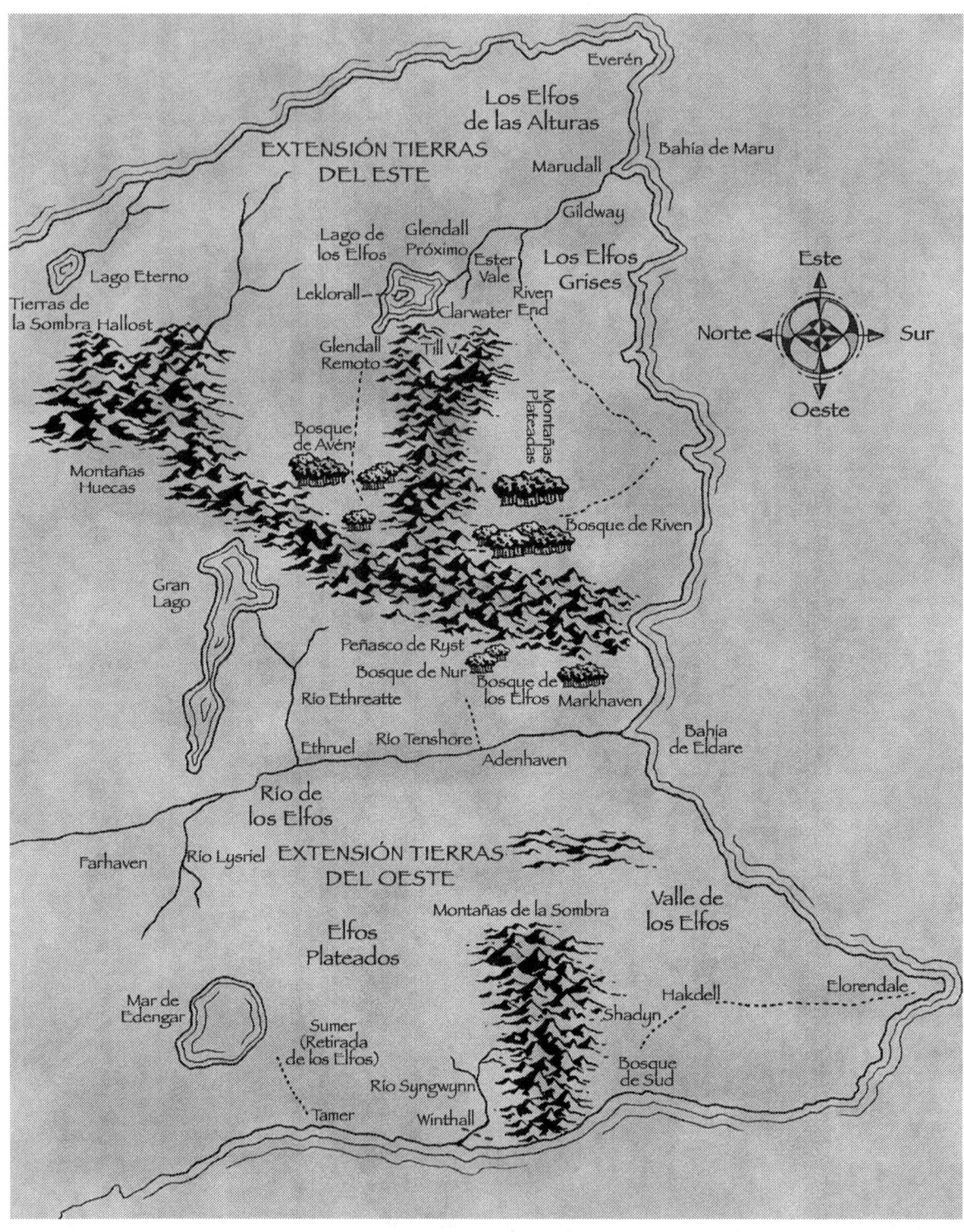

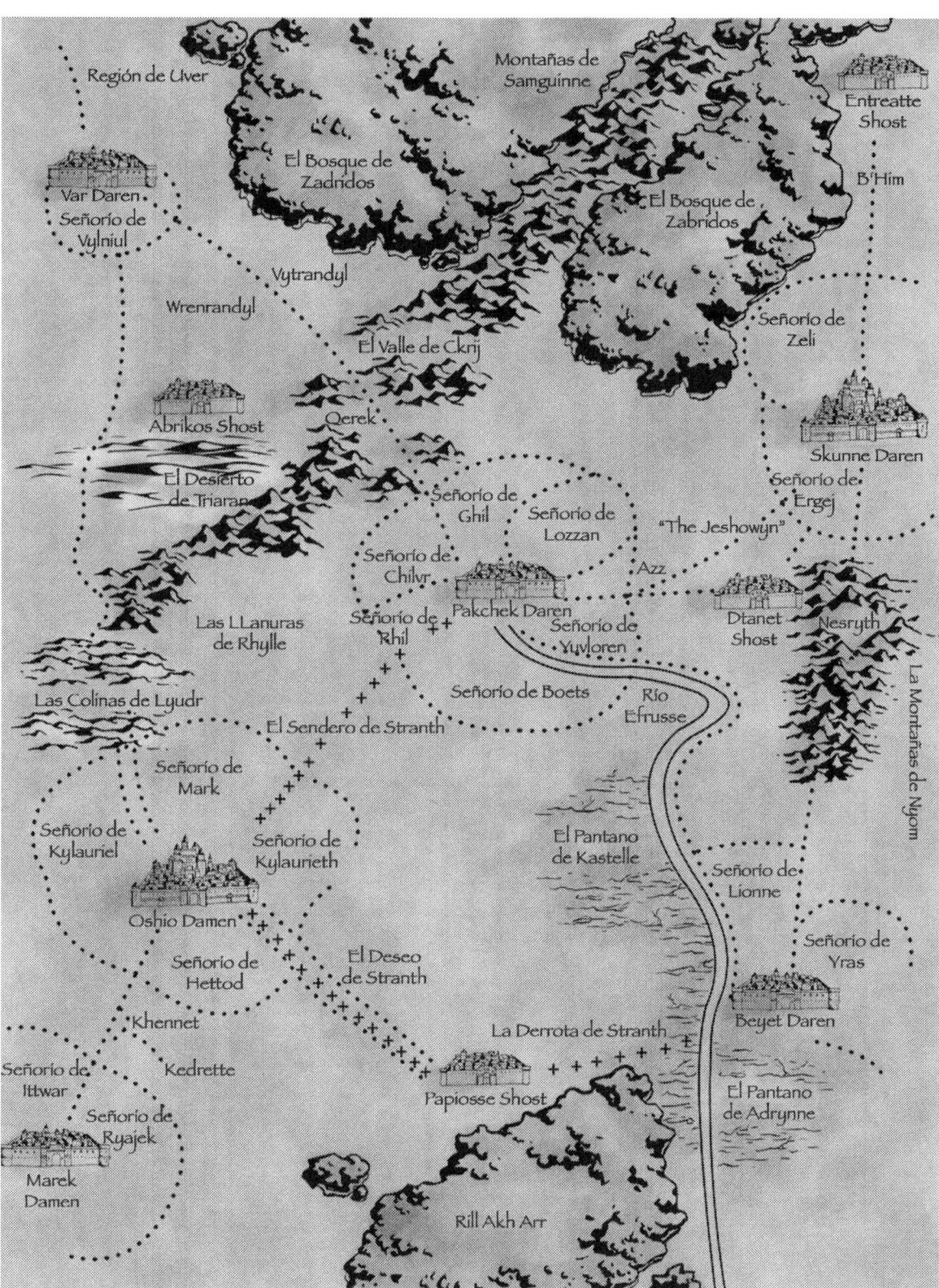

Keeper Martin's Tales

The Kingdoms & the Elves of the Reaches
Inside you'll discover the breathtaking world of Ruin Mist where the mystical and the magical abound, and you'll fall in love with a boy who would become a mage, a princess who is just now seeing the world around her, a warrior elf who undertakes an epic journey, and their friends.

The Kingdoms & the Elves of the Reaches 2
Adrina, Emel, Vilmos, Galan and Seth must survive the greatest challenge Great Kingdom has faced in hundreds of years: the dissolution of the Kingdom Alliance and the battle to save Quashan'. Survival in a changing world depends on their ability to adapt and if they fail, their world and everything they believe in will perish.

The Kingdoms & the Elves of the Reaches 3 & 4
Adrina, Emel, Vilmos, Galan and Seth face even greater challenges as their world is transformed. Vilmos, in his quest to become the first human magus in a thousand years, must control the darkness within him. Adrina must accept her place and work together with Emel to help the elves make their plea to Great Kingdom's council. What happens along the way will amaze you.

In the Service of Dragons

The direct continuation of The Kingdoms & the Elves of the Reaches!

Ruin Mist Tales

For every fantastic story you'll ever find there are often other stories that retell the adventures from different points of view—so why should it be any different in Ruin Mist? Join us now as we walk the dark path through the chronicles of Ruin Mist. Discover new secrets, new dangers, new visions and new realities!

Magic Lands

Following the village elder's advice, Ray leaves his home village, setting out for the place lost and deep where he will find a companion for his journey to the stone land and where he will discover that there is no easy path from childhood to manhood. "Beware lashing tail and gnashing teeth," the village elder warns him, "and if Old Bull doesn't get you, Mother Slither surely will."

Thank you for your purchase! Please visit www.tvpress.com and www.robertstanek.com on the Internet for more information on Robert Stanek and his books.

www.ingramcontent.com/pod-product-compliance
Lightning Source LLC
Chambersburg PA
CBHW051415070526
44584CB00023B/3442